COMMUNICATION AND SOCIAL CHANGE
IN DEVELOPING NATIONS
A CRITICAL VIEW

Communication and Social Change in Developing Nations

A CRITICAL VIEW

Göran Hedebro

THE IOWA STATE UNIVERSITY PRESS / AMES

Göran Hedebro is Doctor of Economics, School of Journalism, University of Stockholm, Stockholm, Sweden. He is also consultant to the Swedish International Development Authority on issues concerning assistance in the field of mass media.

Printed by
The Iowa State University Press
Ames, Iowa 50010

First edition, 1982

Library of Congress Cataloging in Publication Data

Hedebro, Göran, 1945–
    Communication and social change in developing nations.

    Bibliography: p.
    Includes index.
    1. Underdeveloped areas—Communication. 2. Underdeveloped areas—Mass
media. 3. Communication in rural development. 4. Diffusion of innovations.
5. Social change. I. Title.
HB980.H4 1981   30.2.2′ 09172′ 4   81–8191
ISBN 0-8138-0326-8   AACR2

CONTENTS

PREFACE

As a researcher in the field of communication, I have encountered Third World problems in several different contexts. In 1971, while working for the Swedish International Development Authority (SIDA), I studied the difficulties of disseminating health and nutrition information in Ethiopia for the Ethiopian Nutrition Institute, an Ethio-Swedish project. Later I made other studies for SIDA, but they were on information activities directed toward the Swedish public for the purpose of creating greater awareness about underdeveloped countries.

My doctoral dissertation dealt with the role of information for citizens' participation in society. After it was completed in 1976, I was invited to the Institute for Communication Research at Stanford University as a postdoctoral fellow. Stanford is one of the few institutions that runs both advanced courses and research projects on communication and development issues. My year there gave me many opportunities to collect material for this book. It was also a very stimulating time filled with discussions with staff members and students from all parts of the world. Many of my opinions were formed through these talks and I am greatly indebted to all my friends at Stanford. I hope they find the contents of our discussions reflected in the book, directly or indirectly.

After returning to Sweden, I followed the international debate by participating in several conferences representing the Swedish Association for Mass Communication Researchers. I have acted as an advisor to SIDA and some other organizations in Sweden interested in communication and social change in the Third World and have taught these subjects at the School of Journalism, University of Stockholm.

In the preparation of the final manuscript, I received valuable and useful comments from several people. It is my great pleasure to thank the following persons for

their detailed viewpoints and encouragement: Professor
Karl-Erik Wärneryd, Economic Research Institute in Stockholm; Associate Professor Kjell Nowak of the same institute; Professor Herbert Schiller, University of California,
San Diego; Professor Everett Rogers, Institute for Communication Research, Stanford University.

Special thanks go also to Kerstin Bell and Ingrid
Rosenvinge for transforming handwritten outlines into
typescript, to Charly Hultén for the painstaking work of
correcting my interpretations of the English language, and
to J. B. for continual spiritual support.

A last word of appreciation goes to the Swedish Agen-
cy for Research Cooperation with the Developing Countries
(SAREC); to the Economic Research Institute, Stockholm
School of Economics, which provided the funding for this
work; and to the School of Journalism, University of
Stockholm, for assistance in producing the manuscript.

COMMUNICATION AND SOCIAL CHANGE IN DEVELOPING NATIONS
A CRITICAL VIEW

1
Introduction

The significance of information in world society is apparent in several ways. The expression *information explosion* is often used to describe what we are experiencing as flows of messages rapidly increase. The explosion is going on in both industrialized and developing countries. Radio and television stations multiply and increase their hours of transmission, computer techniques provide storage capacities of information heretofore unknown, and electronic innovations are quickly expanding.

Information disseminated by the mass media and other channels is used for a number of different purposes: to convey knowledge of a specific kind, to sell products, to distribute political propaganda. In societies with market economies the senders of information are many. The most powerful ones are naturally large: private corporations, foundations, government and its branches, political parties. This diversity may sometimes give rise to conflicting messages on the same matters. Hence, factors contributing to the information explosion are the efforts of protagonists to counterbalance each other's messages; in Sweden, for example, public agencies produce great amounts of consumer information to balance the claims of advertising.

In the Third World, information has come to occupy a central place in efforts to improve living conditions. This interest is relatively new, dating back about 20 years. The systematic study of information in developing nations can be said to have started in the 1950s with Daniel Lerner's book, *The Passing of Traditional Society* (1958), something of a portal. Since then, questions concerning the role of information in social change have been given increasing attention and research in the field has expanded rapidly.

Among the questions studied most extensively are:

To what extent and how can the mass media contribute to national and local development?

How can mass media and personal contacts be used to persuade large groups in a village, region, or an entire country to adopt new techniques and ideas?

Specifically, how can the media be used for educational purposes? This question refers to all forms of education: extramural--ultramural; formal--nonformal; child--adult.

These generally formulated problems are broad and quite naturally include many more specific ones. But they all begin from the assumption that the media constitute a force in society that in one way or another can influence individuals and the structure of society.

The overall purpose of this book is to analyze questions concerning the role of information in social change in the developing countries. What are the main functions of the media in such contexts--what do they do, what can they do, what can they not do? There is now enough theoretical and empirical groundwork to make a critical analysis of these issues and, as will be shown later, there are valid reasons for doing so.

DEFINITIONS OF BASIC CONCEPTS

Communication is the process whereby someone sends a message to someone else and receives a response. This process may occur on more or less equal bases. When the initiative and ability lie solely with the sender, the result is a one-way flow of messages. An example of this is *mass communication*, where the mass media carry the messages. By its very nature mass communication is:

1. Directed in one way with little or no possibilities for the receivers to respond to the senders/the media.
2. Impersonal; the messages are explicitly formulated to suit a mass of people, not any single person.
3. Simultaneous; a large number of people receive a message at the same time.
4. Public.

Information is a concept that carries several meanings. First of all, it refers to the content of a message; a message can be more or less informative. But information can also denote a one-way flow of messages from a sender to a receiver: "He informed me."

In this book the term *communication* is used generally, to describe situations where messages flow between institutions, people, and media, with or without feedback.

Information is used mainly to denote the contents, but
also in some cases to describe situations where it is
clear there is no exchange of messages at all. These
cases are few, however.
    Social change is the transformation that takes place
in all societies, either gradually or in more dramatic
ways. The process can be evolutionary or revolutionary.
The change refers to alterations in the organization of a
society, in its structure, or in the functions performed
by different groups and units within it. By *society* we
mean nations, regions, villages, or any configuration that
forms a social system.
    Development is a particular form of social change
meaning improved living conditions. But it refers not
only to the change process, it describes also the state of
things at the end of this process; it is also a goal.
    As will be shown in the following chapters, the con-
cept of development is central to any discussion of social
change in the Third World. There is no one generally accepted interpretation of what should be understood by the
phrase *improved living standards*, or by what indicators
the standards should be measured. Thus, in any critical
examination of the functions that various scholars assign
to communication, one must first explicate the underlying
view of development. This we shall do in chapters to come.
In the second part of the book it is contended that development must imply *liberation*, a freeing from all forms
of dependence and oppression.
    Consequently, these two broad definitions mean that
all development is social change, but not all social
change is development. Many cases of social change in the
Third World, and in the industrialized part of the world
as well, do not lead to a better quality of life. Social
change can also be antidevelopment.

LACK OF A DIALOGUE
    Large discrepancies exist between the theoretical
aspects of research concerning communication issues and
their practical applications in development work. Communication research is a relatively new scientific disci-
pline, and comparatively little research has been done.
It is clearly interdisciplinary, drawing on sociology,
psychology, anthropology, political science, and economics, and, regrettably, research findings have not always
been suited to the kind of problems planners and decision
makers face.
    The planner may put his problem this way: How can I
best disseminate information to improve health and nutrition among a population? What can best be achieved with
X amount of money? The kind of advice that is available

from research, however, does not generally discuss the
question in this direct way. Often the problem is put
into a larger perspective and, typically, the conclusion
may be that this question cannot solely be regarded as an
information problem. The solution lies, it is thought,
in building more health centers, educating more qualified
personnel, or improving available medical supplies and
equipment. Quite obviously, these and other related measures might have a more palpable influence on the health
and nutritional status of the people in the country than
any information activity. Such measures must, of course,
be pointed out. But for planners in Ministries of Health,
Community Development, or Education they are of little
help.

    Moreover, studies of relevance to the problem facing
planners may exist, but the question is: To what extent
are the results generalizable from the setting in these
studies? Can a planner in Kenya rely on results obtained
in India? To what extent is there cross-cultural com-
parability?

    The situation described has led to a gap between
decision makers and researchers. As a result, persons
involved in fieldwork and development administration have
turned to one sector of applied communication for practical recommendations, namely, advertising. This is, of
course, rational in a sense, but it seems unfortunate that
such a limited approach to communication has come to exercise so strong an influence in the solving of problems
that quite obviously cannot be attacked with information
alone.

    A second circumstance also has relevance for under-
standing the lack of a fruitful dialogue between decision
makers and researchers, especially in Europe. Many of the
scholars and much of the research in the communication
field are of North American origin. Since the study of
communication in social change became an important issue,
the United States has had an extremely dominant position,
much stronger than in many other scientific disciplines.
This has not favored a dialogue for reasons of geographical distance alone. But other disadvantages stemming
from this situation may have had even more serious
effects. They concern the general view of social change.

    The planning of communication activities as a means
to influence the change process in less-developed countries depends on what is understood by development: What
goals are to be reached by change efforts? As will be
discussed in detail in Chapters 2 and 3, some of the very
first influential works had definite perspectives on this,
which, however, were never quite made explicit. To understand how these scholars saw the causes of underdevelopment and what kind of society they had as their goal, the

implicit or silent assumptions have to be made clear.

It seems that the North American view of communication came to be accepted by many European aid agencies without much critical scrutiny of the development ideology behind it. If an examination had taken place at the beginning, the finding would have been that the development model, of which these communication theories were an essential part, was not necessarily suited to other countries! The United States and Sweden, for example, obviously have quite different views of what development implies and how it should be brought about. They differ in their choice of aid forms (multilateral vs. bilateral) as well as their judgment as to what countries should be given financial assistance, etc.

Thus, the failure of many countries to analyze the ideology implicit in North American development strategies meant the importation of a certain perspective on development, one that was not always in line with the perspective the countries had chosen as their own.

A third point concerns the literature. As noted earlier, communication draws from many areas and thus should be able to contribute to many problem areas. In most development programs an element of knowledge transfer becomes a communication problem. The communication component is often the key to the failure or success of specific development projects. Consequently, improved insights into the problems of communication should increase the chances of success of development efforts in quite different fields: agriculture, health, employment, and technical programs.

This book is not a handbook with practical tips on how to communicate better with people in the developing parts of the world. Instead, the stress is on understanding the role of communication—what it does, what it can do, and what it cannot do. In this way, the book, it is hoped, may lead to the opening up of a dialogue between scholars from various disciplines, and between researchers and development planners/decision makers. The purpose is to arrive at a more critical and more realistic view of what communication means to a society.

However, at present such knowledge transfer is scant. To some extent this is due to the nature of the literature to date. Few books can serve as introductions to the field for persons who have neither much time or interest, but who simply feel they could gain from knowing a bit more. Most of the works in the field are unfortunately long, and they usually deal with quite specialized problems. Hence, it is difficult to get an overview of the field.

At the same time, the mid-1970s has been an exciting period for anyone interested in communication and social

change. It has been a time of reevaluation, in which
established truths have been reexamined in the light of
over 20 years of empirical work. Also, many more scholars
and practitioners now come from Third World countries.
Several of them are extremely critical of what have been
the dominant ideas concerning the use of communication.
They urge the need for models better adapted to *their*
situation, *their* problems, and *their* possibilities to
emerge from underdevelopment. In this situation they look
with great interest to countries following alternative
paths toward development. China, Cuba, and Tanzania are
examples of such nations, and much more is known now
than only a few years ago. The interesting thing is that
successful use of communication activities seems to be one
important explanation for the positive results achieved in
these countries, particularly in family planning, literacy, and rural development. These countries pose a chal-
lenge to the traditional communication models, and have
attracted great interest from other developing nations.

PERSPECTIVES IN THIS BOOK
        The goals of this book are to bridge some of the gaps
mentioned above and to help create a mutual body of
knowledge in the field of communication and social change.
It presents different perspectives on the use of communication, starting from a historical review of some of the
early theories presented. These theories have been and
still are highly influential in the ways the mass media
and other forms of communication have come to be used to
steer the change process in society.

2
How It Began

Social change has always interested and intrigued society.
It is one of the most fundamental characteristics of human
history, and, from both necessity and curiosity, an understanding of the change process has been sought. Necessity
refers to the fact that we have strived from the beginning
to increase our control over our environment. We have
tried to gain more knowledge about it, thereby increasing
the possibilities for arranging it in a way that we our-
selves want. Curiosity reflects another side of us: our
penchant for exploring the unknown for the mere satisfac-
tion of experiencing something new.

The underlying questions are: What makes societies,
nations, villages change? And, What makes people change
their behavior, attitudes, ways of life? Over the years
many scholars from different scientific disciplines have
occupied themselves with these questions, presenting different theories for social change. But, not surprisingly,
no one theory has been accepted by all. Perhaps it is
also wishful thinking to believe that such a theory can
ever be developed. Changes that occur in the twentieth
century may have to be explained by factors and conditions
that did not even exist, say, a thousand years ago. While
there are similarities in social change processes over
time and among cultures, the differences may be just as
important. Theories have to be revised and complemented
as our own societies enter into new stages.

One factor of obvious importance to the change process is communication, the exchanges of messages. Some
may argue that other factors are of much greater importance: for example, ownership of the means of production;
political struggle; the mobilization of class consciousness; capital growth; technical know-how. But, even so,
they agree that no change can occur without flows of information. Communication is very much involved in the
change process, and those who have access to communication

facilities are in a position to exert a strong influence
on the direction the change will take.

From this point of view, it is not difficult to
understand that communication has been given considerable
attention in nations where socioeconomic improvements are
of extreme urgency. This concerns the developing countries but the tendency is the same in industrialized
countries. In Sweden, for example, both the public and
private sectors have increased their communication activities markedly during the last decade. The reason, of
course, is that the dissemination of information is an
important means by which to influence and control the
course taken.

So, although this book deals with the developing
countries, the question of communication and change in
society is by no means solely a Third World problem. It
is a highly general one, with many basic similarities
among all countries no matter what their states of development.

DEVELOPING COUNTRIES: A DEFINITION AND A WORD OF CAUTION

Let us immediately point out that the term *developing
countries* is very misleading in several respects. First
of all, countries in themselves are not wholly underdeveloped. In most nations of the world there are sectors of
society that are quite highly developed and where people
do not suffer from what are commonly referred to as symptoms of underdevelopment: poverty, malnutrition, chronic
disease, unemployment, low income per capita, and a low
rate of literacy. As an example, in the United States,
often considered the most highly developed nation of all,
large groups live under conditions that cannot be more
adequately described than as underdeveloped.

As a contrasting example, some groups in India are
not underdeveloped at all. So, the term *underdeveloped*
or *undeveloped* should rather be applied within countries
to classes and groups in that society or in the world as
a whole. Since, however, the term is frequently used in
debates about social-change problems in Asia, Africa, and
Latin America, there is still reason to use it, but only
*when referring to countries where a majority of the popu-
lation lives under strained conditions of the kind described above.*

Here another problem arises, however. There is no
single standard definition of what countries should be
labeled *developing* and what countries should be labeled
developed. One classification that seems to have acquired
a rather wide acceptance is that made up by the Development Assistance Committee of the Organization for Economic
Cooperation and Development (OECD). Outside Europe, all

countries except the United States and Canada, South
Africa, Japan, China, Australia, and New Zealand are
classified as developing. In Europe, Cyprus, Gibraltar,
Greece, Malta, Portugal, Spain, Turkey, and Yugoslavia are
labeled developing countries.
Other lists exist but differ only slightly from the
one above. What confuses the picture is that other concepts have also been introduced. *Less-developed countries*
(LDCs) is synonymous with developing countries. The term
the Third World has no clear definition but is generally
used to refer to developing countries outside Europe.
Least-developed countries (LLDCs) is a group of twenty-
five nations identified by the UN General Assembly as
being in a particularly difficult situation on three
grounds:

1. They have a per capita Gross National Product
(GNP) of $100 or less.
2. Manufacturing amounts to 10 percent or less of
GNP.
3. Twenty percent or less of persons aged 15 years
or more are literate.

In other words, these are the poorest countries
among the developing nations.
Finally, another subgroup has been designated the
most seriously affected countries (MSACs). This classification was adopted by the UN in 1974 to refer to those
countries that suffered seriously as a result of rises in
the price of oil, food, and other commodities. All but
five of the LLDCs appear on this list. This is another
group of particularly poor countries.
In this book the primary focus is on the developing
countries in Africa, Asia, and Latin America. The expressions *underdeveloped, undeveloped, less developed, Third
World countries,* are used as synonyms, although there are
great differences among them if they are analyzed closely.
"The poorest countries" refers to nations that suffer
extreme symptoms of underdevelopment. But again a word of
caution: The reason countries can be classified as "poor"
is not in most cases that they lack natural resources or
the skill to use them. It is that they have become involved in a dependency situation. As a result of this
relationship these countries have not been able to use
their natural resources for their own national development.
They have been kept in a state of poverty, some countries
more than others. These are really the poorest countries.
Several objections concerning the accepted terminology have been noted. Let us raise one more. There is an
inherent danger in lumping together countries with different historical backgrounds, different geographical con-

ditions, different sizes of population, and so on. The
problems developing countries face are similar, but the
variations among them are so wide that great care must be
taken in suggesting adequate ways to improve their standards of living. Take, for example, the People's Republic
of China, Iran, and Uganda. Is it really meaningful to
describe and analyze the role of communication in these
countries as a group?

The contention here is that it is. There is a common
body of questions about the functions of the media, the
similarity in the technology used, and the institutional
arrangements surrounding the media effects. These concerns can be dealt with in a general way to build a general body of knowledge about the role of communication in
social change processes. But--and this is a key to understanding this book--unless one takes specific national,
regional, or local conditions into account, this understanding can never lead to any sensible practical applications. And, ultimately, this is what research in the
communication field should lead to: a better use of the
media for economic, social, and political development.

THREE LEVELS OF STUDY
For the sake of clarity, we can single out three
different aspects of communication and development. They
correspond also to different levels of analysis.

The first is the approach where the development of
the nation is the focus. How can the mass media contribute to such efforts? Here, the politics and functions of
the mass media in a general sense are the primary objects
of study, as well as problems concerning the organizational structure and ownership and control of the media.
Today the term *communication policy* has come to be used
as a summarizing concept for this group of studies. It is
the broadest and most general of the three, and compared
to the other two areas little research has been carried
out.

The second type of study tries to understand the role
of the mass media in national development but it is much
more specific. The media are seen as educators or teachers. The idea is that mass media can be used to teach
people skills of different kinds and, under some conditions, to influence attitudes and behavior. Often, coordinated efforts such as campaigns are used to accomplish
the objectives. The main question in this group of
studies is the following: How can the media be used most
efficiently to bring a certain kind of knowledge to the
people in the nation?

The third approach is oriented toward change in the
local community or village. It concentrates on the intro-

duction of new ideas, products, and practices and their spread in a village or region. The communication aspects in such studies are considered with reference to the following question, which is essential to the study of innovations: How can communication activities be used to promote widespread acceptance of new ideas and products?

It should be stated that the three approaches outlined here are not sharply separated and, as will be shown in Chapters 2 and 3, they share much the same philosophy in the way the tasks and functions of communication are conceptualized.

MASS MEDIA AND NATIONAL DEVELOPMENT

In the years around 1960 UNESCO paid a lot of attention as to how the press, radio, films, and television could contribute to nation building. Indeed, there seemed to be many indications that economic improvements do go hand in hand with expansion of the mass media. An almost classical study undertaken by UNESCO in 1961 showed the following striking correlations among all the developing countries of Africa, Latin America, the Middle East, and Southeast Asia.

TABLE 2.1. Correlations between Mass Media and Development

Factor	Per capita income	Literacy	Urbanization	Industrialization
		%		
Newsprint consumption per capita	0.83	0.82	0.69	0.68
Daily newspaper circulation per 100 persons	0.83	0.79	0.75	0.51
Cinema seating capacity per 100 persons	0.80	0.68	0.86	0.82
Number of radio receivers per 100 persons	0.86	0.72	0.71	0.78

Source: UNESCO, 1961, p. 17.

The crucial question, however, is: What do the results really mean? Do they imply that mass media can cause the development measured by these indicators? Or is the causal relationship the other way around: Is economic development a necessary prerequisite for, and does it lead to, a well-developed media system? The answer is that the figures prove neither. Like all correlations, they merely show that two events occur simultaneously. Of their mutual relationship nothing can be said. They may be just two different aspects of basically the same change: a more highly developed media structure may be merely another indicator of the kind of economic development the other indicators express.

Then again, there may also be some kind of causal relationship between the media and economic progress. At

the end of the 1950s and in the early 1960s this question
was brought up more explicitly than before. Until then,
communication (here meaning the mass media) had not been
given much attention in established theories of social
change. Economic theories stressed capital accumulation,
growth, investments, and savings. Political theories saw
such factors as power, relations among different groups
in society, elites, and leadership as central. Psychological theories emphasized the need for individual change
and the acquisition of new attitudes and values favorable
to modernization.

Not until this point in time were various aspects of
communication systematically introduced into models for
social change. This thinking was also supported by international bodies. UNESCO, for example, made a concrete
suggestion that every country should aim at a minimum
level of their mass media facilities. The UNESCO standards were, per 100 inhabitants: 10 copies of daily newspapers, 5 radio receivers, 2 cinema seats, 2 television
receivers. According to figures in Frey (1973), around
1960 very few developing countries met these standards.
Many countries were far below.

So it was no small task that UNESCO proposed. But
why were the media considered so essential in the social
change process? In what ways was it claimed they could
contribute to national development?

A Communication Model of Development

In 1964 Wilbur Schramm published *Mass Media and
National Development*, written at the request of UNESCO.
It rapidly became a cornerstone and in many ways it summarizes the thinking of the time among mass media people.
Of course, it does more since it is also research
oriented. Together with Lerner (1958) and Pye (ed., 1963)
it laid much of the groundwork for future research, both
theoretical and applied. These works are still influential.

It seems clear, however, that the research orientation these authors represent has, compared to other
fields, exercised little influence on how the media have
come to be used in the developing world. Journalists,
politicians, and civil servants have probably had the
greatest influence. It is difficult to assess what research has meant for the direction of applied communication activities. Perhaps it is realistic to say that
practice has come first, research afterward, not the other
way around.

At the same time, however, it is clear that research
in different forms is given a larger role today. Research
also has more to offer, since the methods have been considerably refined. But, in the early 1960s when re-

search was young and weak, it was the practitioners who
steered.

The views of Schramm, Lerner, Pye, and some other
scholars became widely accepted partially because they
reflected the views held by media practitioners rather
than the main findings of communication researchers. In
1960 Joseph Klapper published empirical findings that became a milestone in the continuous discussion of media
impact. The conclusion Klapper drew was that the media
have little or no direct effect on people. Rather they
tend to reinforce attitudes and behaviors that people already possess. Their potential for change is small.
Schramm, Lerner, and Pye all claimed more or less the
opposite. In their views media *do* have great potential
for teaching people to behave and think differently. This
was what the media specialists wanted to hear.

How did these scholars formulate their ideas about
development? The key to national development was seen as
a rapid increase in economic productivity. The role of
the media was to mobilize human resources by substituting
new norms, attitudes, and behaviors for earlier ones in
order to stimulate increased productivity. One of the
psychological states of mind given particular attention
was empathy (Lerner, 1958). Empathetic persons were those
having great capacity to relate to new aspects of a changing environment. They have a "rustic personality" and the
capacity to put themselves in others' situations. Closely
related to this is mobility, meaning a high capacity for
change, being future oriented, rational, having augmented
desires coupled with the belief that something can be done
to realize one's aspirations. Lerner argued that this is
the personal style that dominates in modern societies.

Mobility could be experienced directly but also indirectly via the media. The mass media should act as
mobility multipliers. An expanding mass media system,
Lerner argued, spreads attitudes favorable to social
change, and through other mechanisms these ideas will promote development. His model, in its simplest form, can be
illustrated this way:

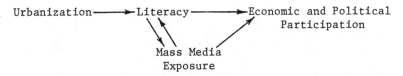

Figure 2.1. Lerner's communication model for development

Increased literacy is assumed to lead to increased
media exposure which in turn should stimulate participation (in this model meaning monetary income per capita),

and voting. Studies in several Middle Eastern countries
led Lerner to see the formation of denser population
groups as a necessary prerequisite for this process to get
under way. He states that increasing urbanization tends
to raise literacy. His model also posits a reciprocal relation between literacy and mass media exposure.
   Another closely related attribute considered important was a motivation to do well, to seek and meet chal-
lenges, and to succeed. McClelland (1961) called this a
"need for achievement," and it was seen as an essential
characteristic of modern persons and modern societies.
Degree of achievement orientation is seen as culturally
determined, being passed on through child-rearing practices and behavioral norms within the family.
   Thus, the first observation is that the task of the
media should be to alter people's psychological or mental
set. People should think in other ways than before. This
particular view of how development is brought about has
been a prominent feature of this tradition ever since. A
recent case in point is Inkeles and Smith (1974) who see
modernization primarily as a question of individual change.
   But there were also other things the media could and
should do.

Other Objectives for the Mass Media

   According to Inkeles and Smith, an important aim of
the media should be to teach the new skills necessary in a
modern society. They identified an enormous need for new
information in all areas of rapidly changing society:
education, agriculture, health, community development,
industrial skills, and literacy. The teaching of new
skills, it was argued, would make people want even more
information, especially once they could read and write;
these were seen as the most important skills of all.
   By establishing a wide-ranging mass media system,
knowledge and skills could be multiplied much more rapidly
and inexpensively than before. The media might compensate
for the lack of teachers, schools, and educational materials (Schramm 1967).
   Furthermore, several authors stressed the importance
of creating a *sense of nation-ness*. Many developing countries are mixtures of different cultures, languages,
political systems, and religious beliefs. This is regarded as a serious obstacle to social change on the national
level. People should be concerned not with improvements
in their own local area only; they must understand the
needs of other villages or areas as well. The presence of
the mass media, it was argued, can expand people's hori-
zons and enlarge their focus of interest to include other
regions besides the local one. Furthermore, the mass
media present possiblities of promoting the use of one

common language for the sake of mutual understanding among various ethnic groups. Not until there is a feeling of concern for the nation as a whole can development be brought about. Only then are people prepared to make sacrifices for others outside the local community.

Some scholars stressed the need for participation by the people in the development efforts and in political decision making. Many projects have evidently failed simply because the people who were to gain from the project were not listened to. Participation may be a necessary precondition for successful attempts to change a nation or to build a nation. Different authors imply varying degrees of participation, but the general idea is the same: a dialogue increases the likelihood that change will be accepted by the people affected.

Others, however, saw communication in this context from a somewhat different perspective. Pye (ed., 1963, p. 229) asserts, for example, that under some conditions communication should rather be used toward an opposite purpose: "In those countries with a small modernized elite the weight of communication policies should be on the side of protecting the freedom of these leaders and strengthening their influences throughout the society." This is a much more directly political view of the role of the media (to defend the elite) but Pye's view seems to be a minority one.

It is important to note, however, that political implications occur in most works. Schramm (1964) points out that communication can be used either as national stimulant or tranquilizer. He makes the important observation that the mere presence of a communication system does not guarantee an improved standard of living for the population. It may even be used to divert attention away from national problems.

But this is also a minority viewpoint. The common focus was on the positive effects that could be accomplished with the assistance of the mass media, not the possible negative effects. Generally there was a very optimistic tone about how communication via the mass media might contribute to social and economic development.

Let us sum up the major functions for communication in a developing society as seen by these and other scholars of that time. More points have been added in this list to underline all the diversified needs communication was supposed to fulfill.

Communication Goals

1. The mass media can create a climate for change by inducing new values, attitudes, and modes of behavior favorable to modernization.

2. The mass media can teach new skills "from
literacy to agriculture to hygiene to repairing a motor
car" (Schramm 1967, p. 18).
3. The mass media can act as multipliers of resources of knowledge.
4. The mass media are unique in the sense that they
can mediate vicarious experiences, thereby reducing the
psychic and economic costs of creating mobile personalities.
5. Communication can raise levels of aspiration
which can in turn act as incentives for action.
6. Communication can make people more prone to participate in decision making in society.
7. Communication can help people find new norms and
harmony in a period of transition (Rao 1966).
8. Communication can change the power structure in a
society of a traditional character by bringing knowledge
to the masses. The informed person takes on greater significance, and traditional leaders whose power is based on
other factors will be challenged.
9. Communication can create a sense of nation-ness.
10. Communication can help the majority of the population realize its own importance, and this may lead to
increased political activity (Rao 1966).
11. Communication facilitates the planning and implementation of development programs that will correspond to
the needs of the population.
12. Communication can make economic, social, and
political development a self-perpetuating process.

A Time of Great Hope
        These various points express the firm belief of the
time that communication could contribute in an important
way to strivings for improved living conditions. The late
1950s and the early 1960s was a time of great hope and
promise.
        To see whether these hopes were founded in reality
we must examine them a bit more in detail, and we must
look not only at what was explicitly stated but equally
at what was not said--the silent assumptions.

What Is Behind the Model?
        Although scholars concerned with the role of communi-
cation in the 1960s differ somewhat in their views, there
is a remarkable consistency among them. Consequently, it
seems right to talk about the birth of one perspective
which has come to exercise a dominant influence in the
field. Let us call it a model, being aware that it does
not qualify as a model in a strictly scientific sense. It
resembles more a number of loosely related proposals and
hypotheses.

The model should be examined with respect to several aspects. The first one is crucial: What does the term *development* really imply, and how is social change to be brought about? One thing is clear. The stress is on economic productivity and economic growth. Gross National Product, total and per capita, are the two most used measures of standard of living. *Development* mainly refers to economic changes and is seen as a shift from a static, agricultural, primitive, rigid, ascriptive society to a dynamic, industrialized, urbanized, rational, and socially mobile nation. These are the terms used. The Western road of social change is explicitly or implicitly understood to be synonymous to development. Other models are either not mentioned or dismissed on the grounds of being totalitarian, unfree, or simply Communist.

The road to being a highly developed nation goes through free enterprise with private ownership, and the stress is on rapid economic growth via industrialization and urbanization. Very little is said, however, about the distribution of the economic growth. The notion is that all citizens will benefit through some trickle-down mechanisms. Exactly how this is going to happen is not made clear, however.

It is obvious that communication scholars at this point in time were heavily influenced in their thinking about development problems by economists, especially Hoselitz (1960) and Rostow (1960). The latter gained prominence for the presentation of a development process divided into five discrete stages: traditional society, establishment of preconditions for takeoff, takeoff into self-sustained growth, the drive to maturity, the age of high mass consumption.

This theory, despite the great attraction of its simplicity, seems to be afflicted with several inadequacies. It also has received criticism from various political quarters. Baran and Hobsbawm (1961) pointed out in a review that in order to solve problems of underdevelopment, one must understand why these countries are underdeveloped. In the stage-theory and consequently also in the communication theories that draw so heavily on this line of thinking, the underdeveloped countries appear almost from nowhere. They have no history; they are just grouped together under a common label: traditional societies.

Excluding history in this way completely overlooks one of the most important causes for underdevelopment. There is ample evidence that the colonization of many countries by Western nations was the beginning of a relationship of dependence that resulted in exploitation. Many examples in history tell how the colonizing country used legislative force to ensure a favorable return for itself and was not the least interested in the development of the colonized nation.

Such relationships have persisted for a great number of years and have not ceased just because of "decolonization." Many newly independent nations are still involved in exploitative relationships with their former colonizers and other politically and economically stronger nations in the world. They are not free to choose their own social and economic systems but must submit to stronger forces in order to survive. Such connections were almost completely overlooked in economic analyses of the early 1960s. Critics, for example, Paul Baran (1957), Baran and Paul Sweezy (1966), and André Gunder Frank (1967) were put aside as pursuing conspiracy theories not in rhyme with reality.

Instead, the causes for underdevelopment were attributed to factors *within* the underdeveloped nations themselves. Such circumstances as disorder in the government bureaucracy, an outdated land tenure system, or inefficient use of available resources were stressed. But what was emphasized most was the general lack of modern facilities--capital, skilled labor, transportation facilities, industrialized production units, and mass media. Much of the blame for the state of the nation was also put on the individual. Citizens, especially the peasantry, were described as tradition bound, fatalistic, prejudiced, and unresponsive to technological innovations or modern ways of thinking.

This way of seeing the problems naturally limited the actions to be taken. The solutions implicit were to induce change by introducing the missing components from outside. Technical aid, human resources, or financial assistance were adequate means by which to create the right preconditions for takeoff. The process of development would then be self-perpetuating and eventually lead to the most developed stage.

Role of the Media: Critical Observations
        The Western bias in the underlying development model is important to observe in several respects. Early theorists took the necessity of free flows of information, a free market economy, free press, and free enterprise system for granted. Both Pool (1963) and Schramm (1964) stated outright that one important function of an expanding communication system was to bring market mechanisms into full swing. Government control in almost any form was seen as hindering development. The skills and attitudes that should be disseminated to the population clearly reflected a certain value system: the Western middle-class life-style. People should possess ideas of better opportunities in life and a belief that these could be realized by individual efforts. As for the "new oppor-

tunities" the media should portray, what the scholars had
in mind was mainly new and better consumer goods.
Here we have the Western model of progress and individual success in a nutshell. Accumulation of consumer
goods and a readiness to acquire more goods when such new
opportunities are opened up by the product development
departments of private enterprises; this is development.
Revealingly enough, the highest stage of national development in Rostowian theory carries the label: "the age of
high mass consumption."
Having established this fundamental bias, the question then becomes whether spreading the mental set and
skills necessary for takeoff really can bring about the
changes hoped for? Part of the answer has been suggested
above.
The development model upon which these assumptions
rests had from the outset excluded some major determinants
to underdevelopment. Hence, recommendations for action
based on the model could not attack such important causes
since they had in effect been defined away as not essential. Instead, the focus fell on new ways of thinking
(modern attitudes) as the prime movers in social change.
This model of national development is strongly rooted
in a psychological theory of change. Pool (1963, p. 249),
for example, suggests that "It is only that kind of internal change in the latent structure of his [the peas-
ant's] attitudes that would produce self-sustaining movement towards modernization."
Examples from history and common sense refute this
simplified view of social change. Individual change is
not unimportant but what seems to be most needed in developing countries are changes in societal structures: land
ownership, ownership of the means of production, distribution of power in political processes, and the like.
These changes are not going to be brought about by using
the mass media to promote such Western middle-class pre-
dispositions as need for achievement, deferred gratifica-
tion, and individual mobility.
This belief in the individual psyche builds to something of an extreme in Lerner's theory of modernization
(Lerner 1958). Lerner's key concept, empathy, the ability
to project oneself into the role of another, becomes the
crucial factor in social change and progress. His model
for development is almost deterministic: once a country
has managed to reach 10 percent urbanization, literacy and
mass media grow with urbanization to about 25 percent.
After this, literacy continues to rise independently of
urban growth. This whole process subsequently leads to an
increased GNP/capita and increased participation in elec-
tions (voting).
The problem here is that this miraculous chain of

events seems most unlikely. The forming of urban centers, education, literacy rates, and growth of mass communication facilities simply cannot be treated as independent antecedents to participation. They are just as dependent on a lot of other circumstances and they are just as much a result of a causal chain in the opposite direction from that posited in Lerner's model. Participation in policy making and the outcome of this process are among the factors that determine the degree of urbanization and the resources allocated to education, media systems, and literacy efforts.

The Communication Model in Its Contemporary Context

As the analysis has shown, the main communication approach at the beginning of the 1960s, when the field of communication and development got under way, can be criticized on several counts. Both the formulation of the problems and the solution suggested were biased so that only a very narrow part of the problem could be met.

Some may find it unfair to criticize ways of thinking brought forward 15 to 20 years ago and to evaluate them from a position of today. But the scientific process is fundamentally critical. Old theories are criticized and revised in the light of empirical evidence and other experiences. This process then repeats itself over time. Criticism and new ways of looking at a problem constitute necessary and essential components of research.

Moreover, the critique is of a general kind, and not actually based on new experiences of the late 1970s. Those points of criticisms might very well have been expressed much earlier. Indeed, they were, but they were not given great attention since they came from scholars outside the bounds of what was considered "normal science."

To understand theories one has to look also at the historical and political context at the time they were introduced. Such a perspective can explain why certain ideas were prominent at a particular point in time. The views of communication and development discussed here have an important connection back to the end of World War II. Europe was in ashes and the Americans were the celebrated liberators. To get Europe back on its feet again the Marshall Plan was devised and many countries received technical and financial assistance. Although this plan was criticized many European countries made remarkable progress in a relatively short time. The faith in technology as a tool for rapid social change in a positive sense was strengthened. Obviously, it seemed to have worked well in the United States and in Europe.

When the poor countries in Africa, Asia, and Latin America began their struggle for independence and improved living conditions, it was in a sense natural to carry on

in the same way that had recently proved to be so promis-
ing. Thus, the assistance extended to the developing
world was heavily influenced by the successful transfer
of technology, capital, ideas, and organizational setup
that took place between the United States and Europe. Why
would not this approach work for other countries with
similar problems?

The developed countries had long held advantageous
positions vis-à-vis the developing world. Raw material
prices had been kept low, the conditions of trade having
been dictated by the industrialized nations. The 1960s
was the first decade of actual liberation for the poor
countries. Not surprisingly, the developed nations tried
to appear humanitarian, allowing independence or liberation
while at the same time guarding their politically and
economically favorable positions. Western countries more
or less actively supported endeavors directed toward maintaining pro-Western ways of development in the Third
World. The philosophies and practical recommendations in
much of the communication literature of the first half of
the 1960s were no exceptions in this regard. On the contrary, they were strongly supportive of the Western, capitalist development model and just as much as this communication approach was formulated for the sake of urgent
social change in the developing part of the world, it was
also formulated to preserve existing international relationships. Another way of putting it is to say that the
communication philosophy was one of several measures that
had to be taken to find new forms for maintaining the exploitative relationship. For many Western nations, probably most obviously for the United States, technical and
financial aid are very closely associated with foreign
policy. In fact, assistance *is* an important part of this
policy.

This is not to say that individual researchers working in the field of communication and development were
steered by such motives. But the fact cannot be overlooked that the dominant communication model was and is
favorable to the developed nations. The industrialized
countries never were regarded as causes for underdevelopment; they were looked upon as the ideals and as donors of
hardware and software in mass media activities.

It is also in this light we should see the general
unwillingness to even consider other roads to development
than the Western one. Of course, to some extent this is
because so little was known about what was happening in
other parts of the world. But the Western position did
not stop at mere ignorance; other efforts to break the
bonds of underdevelopment were strongly denounced. The
reporting from the People's Republic of China, Cuba, and
the Eastern European countries are striking examples of

this. Thus, yet another illustration of the close links
between foreign policy and development aid is provided.

Practical Implications

It should be kept in mind that the criticism expressed here did not receive general attention until much
later. The dominant model rapidly won wide acceptance
over the world. It came to exert great influence over the
use of communication activities in developing countries.
But, as noted earlier, media practitioners and government
decision makers had already settled on this direction and
use for the media. When research came along and formulated these views in more scientific language, it served
only as a legitimization of how the media were already run.
The recommendations from UNESCO about a minimum level
of mass media facilities have been mentioned. From the
early 1960s on, both technology and ideas were absorbed
by developing countries from Europe and North America.
Foreign advisors made plans for journalism training programs and the building of mass media facilities.
This optimistic view of communication was widely incorporated in aid programs, and information has since been
used in many different contexts. Programs of literacy,
agricultural extension, community development, health, and
nutrition are all areas where the transfer of certain
skills, attributes, or knowledge has been seen as central.
Generally speaking, the early 1960s was the beginning of a
period where this model was to be tested empirically in
the developing part of the world.

ADDITIONAL READINGS:
Elliot, P., and Golding, P., 1974, "Mass Communication and
      Social Change: The Imagery of Development and the
      Development of Imagery." In de Kadt, E., and
      Williams, G. (eds.): *Sociology and Development*.
      London: Tavistock Publications.
Frank, A. G., 1969, *Capitalism and Underdevelopment in
      Latin America*. New York: Monthly Review Press.
Golding, P., 1974, "Media Role in National Development:
      Critique of a Theoretical Orthodoxy." *Journal of
      Communication*, 24(3):39-53.
Rogers, E. M. (ed.), 1976, *Communication and Development:
      Critical Perspectives*. Beverly Hills, Calif.: SAGE
      Publications.

3

Communication and the Diffusion of Innovations

The large number of village studies in anthropology indicate a high degree of interest in small societal units.
In studies of social change at the village level particular attention has been given to the impact of the introduction of new objects or new ideas. A new tool means not
only that the society has acquired a more efficient way of
solving a practical problem; it may also imply other
changes. The introduction of this new object may bring
about changes in the established social organization.
Traditional authorities and ways of thinking may be
threatened, and a need arises to establish a social order
better adapted to the new products and ideas.
An important conclusion from the anthropological
field seems to be that objects and ideas brought in from
outside exert greater influence on a culture than factors
emanating from within the culture itself. It is for this
reason anthropological studies focus to such an extent on
contacts between cultures and the transformation of new
objects as they enter a new culture. This focus is commonly referred to as the study of cultural diffusion.
Change, in the sense of the introduction of new
things, has been actively promoted in different parts of
the world. A prime example is in the field of agriculture
in the United States where the introduction and acceptance
of new ideas has long been the essence of domestic policy
for reaching increased productivity. This is true for
many other countries as well, but the United States seems
to have been particularly successful in this respect,
consequently, a lot of experience has been accumulated.
From such results a general theory has been constructed,
and it is of interest here that communication has been
assigned a large and important role. The underlying question has been and still is: How can communication activities be designed to increase the chances of acceptance of
new products or ideas by large groups in the population?

BASIC CONCEPTS IN DIFFUSION THEORY
     In 1962 Everett Rogers published a book that summa-
rized several years of empirical studies in the United
States concerning the introduction and spread of new
ideas. This led to a general theory that has become extremely influential in developed and developing nations.
It is necessary to look into some of the central concepts
used there; the role and tasks given to communication can
then be analyzed.
     Figure 3.1 shows the typical curve of adoption of an
innovation over time. The example is taken from Nypan
(1970) who studied how people in Northern Tanzania adopted
use of a copper oxide spray to protect coffee plants
against insects and diseases.

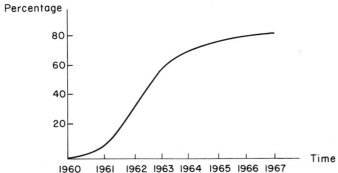

Fig. 3.1. Adoption curve of use of copper oxide
to protect coffee plants

     The figure shows a typical S-pattern, reflecting the
fact that adoption begins slowly, then increases more or
less rapidly, and finally fades off again when some point
of maturity is reached. In the example, it seems that
about 80 percent of the farmers chose to use the copper
spray to increase the yield of coffee. Further, it took
about 7 years from the time the first farmer started
to use spray until the last one did so. Some 20 percent
still have not followed the majority. They may adopt at
an even later stage, although the curve seems to level
off, indicating that the maturity point is around 80 percent.
     In the theory, five groups of adopters, *adopter cate-
gories*, are distinguished according to how early or how
late they adopt an innovation.

     1. *Innovators*, those who adopt first of all. The
first 2.5 percent counted from the left of the S-curve.
     2. *Early adopters*, the next 13.5 percent.

3. *The early majority*, the next 34 percent.
4. *The late majority*, the next 34 percent.
5. *Laggards*, the last 16 percent.

These categories show some systematic differences. Several studies have found that earlier adopters generally are younger, have a higher social status, and are better-off financially than the other groups. They often also have had greater mass media exposure and better contact with extension agents. Furthermore, they seem to have higher aspirations than categories who adopt at a later stage.

Many of the results concerning differences between groups adopting an innovation at earlier or later stages in the diffusion process are in many ways self-evident. To find out about the new insect sprays available, a person has to have contact with some source of information, for example, an extension agent. In this work the latter often turns to persons who are interested in new products. Innovations often cost money and involve risk taking, which only the relatively well-off are able to afford. These groups are also the better educated members of society. Looking at the problems from a general sociological perspective, these results are obvious and more or less expected.

There are also other elements in the innovation diffusion theory. One important factor is the characteristics of the new product itself and what they mean with respect to the possibilities of widespread acceptance. Rogers and Shoemaker (1971) use the following scheme to distinguish the characteristics of a product or idea.

1. *Relative advantage* is the degree to which a new idea or product is judged to be superior to something else used earlier.
2. *Compatibility* is the degree to which an innovation is perceived to be in line with existing values or structures within a society.
3. *Complexity* is the degree to which an innovation is difficult to understand or use.
4. *Trialability* is the degree to which an innovation may be tried out on a small scale.
5. *Observability* is the degree to which an innovation yields results that are visible to others.

Any one factor, or a combination, may be crucial to the successful introduction of a given product or technique. To return to the case of the insect spray, it may be a type of innovation that is relatively easy to introduce. The advantages of using it can be shown by comparing the yields from one field prepared with the insecticide and one without. It may also be relatively easy to

use and not require much special training to be handled in
a proper way.
    But these factors alone do not guarantee successful
introduction. Cultural norms and values have to be taken
into account. What is the general attitude toward using
chemicals in agriculture? What is the opinion among
formal and informal leaders, and do any powerful groups in
the village oppose the use of this particular kind of
product? In the example, there seems to have been no such
resistance. On the contrary, leaders were more eager than
others to accept the copper oxide. This, of course, increased the chances of acceptance by a majority of the
farmers. In fact, a positive attitude among the leaders
in the community may be the most important explanation of
the high rate of adoption.
    But there are many cases of more complex innovations
where the outcome is much more uncertain. Let us consider
one in the field of nutrition, the object of a lot of efforts in development work today. It concerns a product
and an idea in one, and illustrates the difficulties implied in the five points above in introducing new and
alien ways of thinking and behaving.

The Case of FAFFA
    In the field of health, particular efforts usually
are made to better the nutritional situation of preschool
children. The problem is that children often go directly
from breast milk to adult food, which may be very meager
for the growing child who needs vitamins and minerals. In
Ethiopia, as in many other countries, a supplementary
children's food was produced. It was a powder to be mixed
with water to make a nutritious porridge. The name given
to the product was FAFFA which in Amharic means "to grow
big and strong." The porridge powder was sold throughout
the country, and agents were engaged to handle the promotion and distribution.
    However, there were great difficulties in reaching
sales figures of any substantial level. Without getting
into all the problems that were encountered, let us consider the reasons why the project met limited success in
terms of the scheme above.
    First, the relative advantage of the product was dif-
ficult to grasp. The porridge was supposed to replace the
leftovers from the head of the household's dinner. It was
difficult for people to see why spending part of the family's income on this porridge might be a good investment.
Why was it really necessary?
    Second, it is clear that in many parts of Ethiopia
this manner of giving children special food meant a radical departure from tradition. As if the mother's breast

milk and the ordinary food prepared in the family were not
good enough!
    A third factor also applied: making the porridge re-
quired boiling water. Quite naturally, this posed special
problems for many families. In addition, there were the
instructions on how to prepare the porridge. Some smaller
studies revealed that many mothers had misunderstood the
directions for use that were taught at health clinics or
the instructions on the bags. Or they had understood the
directions correctly, but had their own beliefs as to how
these should be altered. For example, children were commonly fed too small portions, were fed at irregular intervals, or already-made porridge was stored in such a way
that it became contaminated.
    In one sense, of course, the product was trialable:
everyone could feed their children the porridge. But
again, this meant an expense and people in Ethiopia possess very little cash. So, in reality, only the somewhat
better-off families had a chance to buy it.
    Finally, what about observability? The parents hard-
ly knew what to expect from using the porridge, so, what
should they observe? No dramatic health improvements
could really be promised. The addition of a supplementary
food alone could not dramatically change the frequency of
diseases, child mortality, the psychological and physical
behavior of the child. So, many other factors would have
to be changed in order to make the health situation markedly better. So, even if a family were able to buy the
product, the changes in the child observable to them would
most likely be minor. Why should they use the product at
all if it did not offer them any clear and visible advantages? The little money the family possessed could surely
be better spent some other way.
    This is just one example of an innovation that did
not succeed on a large scale. Many others of various
kinds have been rejected for similar reasons.

THE ROLE OF COMMUNICATION
    As the discussion above suggests, there may be great
difficulties involved in promoting the use of new ideas
and products. One way to increase the probability of
widespread acceptance, according to proponents for this
approach, is the systematic use of communication. The
primary purpose and implication of communication here is
to provide individuals and groups with information that
makes them interested in the innovation.
    Rogers and Shoemaker (1971) describe the four steps
in the innovation decision process that an individual
passes through.

1. The individual is exposed to the existence of the innovation and gains some understanding of how it functions.
2. The individual forms a favorable or unfavorable attitude toward the innovation.
3. The individual makes a choice, whether to adopt or to reject the innovation.
4. The individual seeks reinforcement for the decision he has made. He may, however, reverse his previous decision if exposed to new, contrary information or experiences.

One important point is that at each stage the individual collects information from various sources, but the different sources vary in importance depending on where in the decision process the individual is. For example, the mass media are of greater significance in the first step than they are later. The mass media may have a unique property in their ability to make things known to the public, but when a person makes up his mind about what to think of a new product, he will more likely turn to other people: family, friends, or neighbors. Together they form his net of interpersonal channels, and he can discuss the new thing he has experienced with them. One cannot discuss with the mass media.

Another consistent research finding is that mass media channels are relatively more important than interpersonal channels for early adopters than for late adopters. To some degree this is not a surprising result. When an early adopter adopts a new product, there is no one else around him who has any experience with the innovation. When a late adopter makes his decision, a lot of people can tell him about the product.

But this finding also expresses something more: innovators are oriented toward change; they are looking for new opportunities that may improve their situation. Hence, the information they get from the mass media may be enough to lead them through the whole decision process to a decision to adopt the innovation. People who adopt at a later stage rely more on personal contacts. In the diffusionist perspective, these groups are less change-oriented.

Communication at the Village Level

The basic idea is that some new favorable product or idea exists, and that its acceptance will be advantageous to the individual and/or the village. The task of the change agent working in a region or village is to promote wide adoption, and in this work he has to rely heavily on information. If any major positive outcome is to be expected the agent has to engage in a dialogue with the peo-

ple living in the village. He has to listen to their
problems and to adapt his efforts to how well equipped the
people are to make use of the product in question.
   One essential thing that the change agent must do is
to identify the local leaders. The leaders may base their
authority on different grounds: religious, traditional,
political, but often, new ideas cannot be introduced without the support of such groups. If they do not wish to
encourage the practice of a new idea actively, at least
they should be persuaded not to actively oppose it. The
situation can never be completely brought under the change
agent's control, however. He may find that while his
ideas meet no open resistance, they get no direct support
either.
   Thus, there are many possible barriers to a wide acceptance of a new idea. Sometimes the real obstacles to
the innovation become known only after it has failed.
Take the concept of family planning and the use of contra-
ceptives as an example. Seen from outside the concept
seems sound. People are poor, resources are limited; consequently, people would be better off having fewer children to rear. But seen from the "client's perspective,"
having many children is completely rational. For one
thing, it increases the chances that there will be children left when the parents get old and unable to work for
their own subsistence. Moreover, it means additional
workpower in the household once the children reach a certain age. So why should the concept of family planning be
supported if nothing more is done to improve the living
conditions in the village? These are very plausible explanations for the failure of such an idea. Of course,
other more direct explanations may be influential. For
example, in many cultures, talking about matters that relate to sexual behavior is very offensive. It breaks a
taboo, and for this reason alone people may not pay attention to what the change agent is saying. At first they
may be extremely shocked by the fact that anyone dares
talk about such things at all.
   Although the risks for failure are great, without
communication there is little hope for the acceptance of a
new idea. Accordingly, several research studies have concentrated on this matter. A most well-documented finding
concerns the usefulness of *media forums*. A typical example is the radio forum, where farmers or other groups meet
regularly to listen to a broadcast concerning some aspect
of community development. They then discuss the issues
the program has brought up. The subsequent discussion is
often led by an extension agent or some other person who
has special knowledge of the problem.
   This communication technique was used in the 1960s in
India, Nigeria, Ghana, Malawi, Costa Rica, Brazil, and

some other countries. The forum technique utilizes the
advantages of the mass media and it profits from having a
group discussion. Collective learning and decision making
can create more stable attitude changes than individual
actions. Group pressure in situations like these may tend
to confirm attitudes. This again may result in a generally more favorable attitude toward the innovation, although
in some cases the opposite may also occur. It depends on
the opinions expressed by group leaders.

Communication in the village can occur naturally in
many other ways. The change agent develops a lot of personal, informal contacts with farmers and village leaders.
These contacts may often prove to be most important to the
agent in getting a certain idea or technology accepted.

TRANSFER OF THE UNITED STATES' EXTENSION MODEL

These, then, are the basic ideas in innovation diffusion theory. As has been said, the theory draws on
experiences from several fields, but through the systematic data collection undertaken in North American rural
and medical sociology, they have been integrated into a
more general framework. When the theory was presented in
the early 1960s, it quickly gained attention from scholars
and field workers involved in social change in the developing countries.

The number of studies concerning the spread of innovations increased rapidly as many developing nations found
this theory of change very attractive. They turned to the
United States and other industrialized nations for more
practical advice on how to convert the theoretical aspects
into guidelines for action.

The answer to the need of practical advice was found
in the United States' agricultural extension model. This
model offered a set of practical rules for increasing
agricultural productivity by encouraging the use of new
technology. As in many other Western nations, the number
of people employed in agriculture in the United States has
declined quite drastically and yet total output has multiplied. The extension model in the United States has the
reputation of being successful. It is obviously well organized, and a characteristic of the model is its reliance
on a net of agents and advisory groups. The extension
agent is the key person to bring information about new
machinery, tools, seeds, fertilizers, and financial arrangements to farmers.

In the first half of the 1960s this model was ex-
ported from the United States for use in countries of
Africa, Asia, and Latin America. Many Americans and American institutions/universities were brought in as advisors

and soon extension programs were under way in many developing nations.

Several of the programs begun at this time have been well documented. Let us look briefly at one such project, probably the largest ever to be carried out. The study was executed in three countries simultaneously—Brazil, Nigeria, and India—during the period 1964-1968. The total budget for the study was $1.25 million, and data were gathered from over 10,000 respondents in a total of 255 villages. The project, which resulted in 25 voluminous reports, is summarized by Rogers, Ascroft, and Roling (1970).

The prime objective of the project was to look at how different kinds of innovations were accepted and to characterize the people who used these new ideas and practices. In what ways were they different from nonadopters? How can such knowledge be used to make nonadopters more favorable toward innovations in future programs?

Farmers in the villages were asked if and when they had adopted fertilizers, new crop varieties, improved poultry and livestock breeds, new agricultural equipment, or farming practices. Respondents were also asked about new practices of a more general nature in the area of health: vaccinations, latrine constructions, safe drinking water, modern childbirth practices. Several questions were also asked about information habits: How did the farmer learn about these things?

Not surprisingly, it was found that early adopters, compared to late adopters, were younger, that they had a better education, that they were more cosmopolitan, that they had a greater exposure to the mass media. They were also to a certain extent opinion leaders, in other words, they were asked for advice by other people. The results were quite consistent throughout the three countries involved in the study and were thus accorded considerable generalizability.

CRITICISM AGAINST THE DIFFUSIONIST APPROACH

Although criticism had been raised against the diffusionist approach from its beginning, it was not until the end of the 1960s that it was given any noteworthy attention. This, we note, is the same pattern as was reflected in the preceding chapter concerning the dominant model on communication and national development. The extension model aroused a high degree of optimism among decision makers and scholars, most of whom came from the industrialized part of the world.

When the criticism was finally voiced loud enough to be heard, it attacked several cornerstones of the model.

The first point of criticism questioned the content of the concept "development" and how it was brought about. The following quotation is typical of the view of innovation scholars (Rogers and Shoemaker 1971, p. 11):

> Development is a type of social change in which new ideas are introduced into a social system in order to produce higher per capita incomes and levels of living through more modern production methods and improved social organization. Development is modernization at the social systems level.

Thus, we find the same development philosophy as is present in the model of media and social change at the national level. What the developing countries need to get out of their states of underdevelopment are new technologies, new products, new values, and a new social structure. These things already exist in the developed countries. Consequently what has to be done is to transfer these missing components to the less-developed countries.

But does this really break the bonds of underdevelopment in the village? Hardly, according to such scholars as Frank (1969), Grunig (1971), Felstehausen (1973), and other critics cited in Chapter 3. The main reason for underdevelopment is, they argue, the exploitative relationtionship between industrialized and poor nations. Further, development does not mean going ahead on a Western road of change with a stress on material welfare. The stage of "high mass consumption" that Rostow (1960) posited as the most developed stage for a nation was more a nightmare in many people's eyes than a highly desired goal.

One of the first critics who received some recognition in the communication field was Inayatullah (1967), who stressed the need for alternative perspectives on development. These should reflect the search for ways of life where the goals are not simply to catch up with cultures that measure standards of living along a few dimensions only. Development in his terms becomes something different (p. 101): "it is a process through which a society achieves increased control over the environment, increased control over its own political destiny, and enables its component individuals to gain increased control over themselves."

In such a perspective the introduction of products and ideas of Western origin can hardly be considered equivalent to legitimate development. Such transfer is a kind of imitation and does not release the creative energy the "receiver" needs. Even if non-Western countries might achieve some material development by successful imitation, they would not make any contribution to the culture of humankind.

Reliance on outside influence of this kind has other disadvantages as well. It creates a dependence on the part of the receiver, a dependence indeed opposite to the ideas of self-control and self-reliance.

Proinnovation Bias

Another point of criticism concerns the silent assumption in the diffusionist approach that all innovations are good and should be adopted by everyone. We can all think of many examples of innovations people would be better off not adopting. Bottle feeding is one such example, the use of supplementary milk powder is another. They both replace something clearly more nutritious and involving less risk of infection--the mother's breast milk. These innovations may have a place in a developed society where families have access to pure water, live under hygienic conditions, and generally have larger incomes. But in countries where conditions are quite different, new practices like these cannot be said to improve living conditions for the large majority.

The proinnovation bias not only relates to the individual's adoption or rejection of a certain product. There may be instances when the acceptance of a new idea may lead to unexpected and undesirable consequences, so that the net result for the village or the society as a whole is negative. Many of the innovations introduced in the agricultural field, for example, have been of such a capital-intensive nature that only farmers who already are relatively well-off have had the financial means to adopt the new machinery, new seed, or fertilizer.

The introduction of such innovations has led to increased gaps among various socioeconomic groups. What has been called the Green Revolution in India is an example of this, and there are many other examples in various parts of the world. The principle at work here is old and simple: those who have something from the outset can more easily obtain more of the same and related objects than can others. This does not mean that the poor automatically fall into an even worse situation, but, relatively speaking, the gap between them and the better-off groups grows wider.

The question here, though, is to what extent such results really have come unexpectedly. The Green Revolution outcome is no surprise. Landowners get more wealth, and the landless have to move to the cities in an increasing number, as capital-intensive technology replaces human labor. This, in fact, is an explicit part of the development philosophy of several countries in the Third World. In other cases, however, the social consequences of the introduction of something new into a village have not been clearly foreseeable.

The conclusion to be drawn is that the innovations
approach has pursued the idea that innovations are good
for everyone, paying little attention to social consequences. Only a few consequences have been accounted
for--increased yields, increased productivity, and similar
economic criteria--while many other equally vital factors
have been disregarded.

Ignoring Social Structure
     As in works dealing with the role of the media in
national development, in the diffusionist approach also
there is a tendency to put the blame for underdevelopment
on the individual in the developing society. This tendency means that the farmer is seen as the main obstacle to
development, particularly when he is unresponsive to innovations. Again, this is a psychologization of problems.
In a survey of the literature on this subject, Beltran
(1976) found thirteen personality traits used to describe
the farmer in developing countries. According to these
texts, the farmer possesses the following characteristics:
traditionalism, fatalism, no future orientation, low need
for achievement, lack of entrepreneurship, passivity,
resignation or conformity, lack of risk-orientation, no
thriftiness, superstition, lack of creativity, submissive-
ness, distrust. Beltran continues (p. 354):

> To me this is a Dorian Gray portrait. If rural peo-
> ple in my region have all these traits, or at least
> several of them, I give up as a communication spe-
> cialist working to change anything in them. It would
> be just impossible.

There are other opinions on what factors explain
innovativeness, that is, whether a person is inclined to
adopt a new idea. Several scholars, for example, point to
the crucial influence of social structure on individuals
and their behavior. But as Havens (1972), Grunig (1971),
and Beltran (1974) all show, such aspects have been neglected in the diffusionist approach. Felstehausen (1973,
pp. 42-43) draws the following conclusion:

> The tendency to equate communication problems with
> problems in disseminating technical information has
> led many extension and assistance agencies to virtu-
> ally ignore social and institutional structures in
> promoting development. This is even the case in
> areas where field workers and educators realize that
> information alone cannot change local conditions.

More specifically, the critique points out an implicit assumption in the diffusionist approach that the farmer

has access to information and makes his own decision. But
all individuals occupy a position in a social class structure, and this position largely determines their innovative behavior. Consequently, it is no surprise to find
that persons with larger farms, higher incomes, better
education, and higher exposure to mass media are the ones
to adopt early. They may even be the *only* adopters. Persons with these characteristics have the necessary prerequisites for adoptions; their social position is favorable.

The introduction of new products has to take the social structure into account in two different ways. First,
structural factors can and should be analyzed: Why do
certain groups come to adopt and others do not? Second,
the reverse process should also be studied: How will the
introduction of certain new ideas and products influence
the social structure?

This, then, is the structural perspective that must
be used when studying the individual's adoption or rejection of an innovation. Only then will we in a real sense
understand the farmer's decision, and only then will we
understand the consequences of his decision for the village, the region, or the nation as a whole.

Methodological Shortcomings

Certain weaknesses in the empirical studies of the
spread of innovations render the results somewhat doubtful. Rogers (1976, p. 212) points to some of them. One
is that the propensity to be innovative is measured with
recall data about past adoption behavior, while the factors that are used to explain this are measured in the
present tense. This problem of time-order is referred to
as "yesterday's innovativeness." "It is impossible for an
individual's attitude, formed and measured now, to cause
his adoption of an innovation three years previously...."

Second, in most studies in this tradition, the unit
of analysis is the individual. Almost all data come from
interviews with farmers or questionnaires completed by
individual farmers. But, as noted, other factors, too,
should be used to explain innovative behavior. The structural aspect mentioned earlier is one of these. Another
is the individual's interrelationships and contacts with
other people. Nor have we studied collective decision
making, which is common in developing countries. Many
innovations require collaborative efforts and it is the
group rather than the single individual who makes the
decision.

A third and final comment should be made about the
way research has been carried out. Most diffusion studies
are quite similar both in design and concepts. To apply a
term from the field itself: there have been few innova-

tions in the study of innovations! In a sense this has
made it easier to make generalizations about the findings,
but at the same time it seems to have brought about a
limited understanding of communication programs at the
local level.

The scope and definition of the problems have been
much too narrow. This has led to a static repetition of
almost identical studies in only slightly different national settings. With the large number of surveys carried
out, a high degree of certainty in the findings has been
won, but at the price of little exploration of factors
outside the established borders of the tradition.

4
Uses of Communication for Development

As has been pointed out, a hopeful and optimistic outlook concerning the use of mass media and other ways of disseminating information was evident in the early 1960s. It was hoped that the media would underscore many reforms at both national and local levels that would lead to improved living standards. In the 1960s much effort was devoted to strengthening media facilities. A general effort was made to reach at least the United Nations' minimum figures, and preferably to even surpass them.

DECADE OF THE TRANSISTOR?
Although countries chose to invest differently--more in some media and less in others--the decade saw a general expansion of radio broadcasting. It is a comparatively inexpensive medium. It also has the great advantage of being able to reach far out into villages without a costly transmitter-receiver system.
Statistics for the period show a marked increase in the number of radio receivers in developing regions. According to UNESCO figures (UNESCO 1975) the possession of radio receivers tripled between 1963 and 1973. In Latin America, for example, the number of radios more than doubled in these 10 years. At the same time the population increased too, so the net result, measured as the number of receivers per 1,000 inhabitants, is not quite as high. But, irrespective of how the statistics are expressed, radio stands out over other media in its growth. Wilbur Schramm (1967, p. 3) concludes without any hesitation: "It has been the Decade of the Transistor!" He also estimates that about one-third of all the people in the developing nations have direct access to radio broadcasts.
But it is something of an oversimplification to say that the last part of the 1960s and the early 1970s belonged to one medium. Radio is probably not the medium

that has been allocated the largest sums of money, and
many planners seem to be working on the assumption that
television, not radio, is the medium that can bring about
the greatest changes through the combination of sound and
visual material. It should also be noted that the number
of newspaper copies and cinema seats per thousand persons
has remained largely unchanged.

The figures on the structure of mass media in developing countries taken together are not very encouraging.
Few developing countries today pass the minimum standards
that the UN formulated in 1961, and the rates of change
during the 1960s give no indications that they are about
to pass them. But what is probably most disappointing is
the fact that the gap between the developed and the developing part of the world is increasing.

In Africa, for example, the number of radio receivers
per 1,000 inhabitants has increased, but in the United
States, Canada, and Western Europe it has increased even
more. The same comparison can be made for television and
the outcome is similar. The parts of the developing world
that seem to have built up the strongest mass media structures are the Latin and Central Americas. Their media
figures are still much below the levels of Europe and
North America, however.

MASS MEDIA SYSTEM AT WORK

But statistics are only one aspect of the picture.
The central issue is how the media have been used, for
what purposes and with what results.

The first thing to be noted, then, is that the media
have been used in accordance with the philosophy outlined
in Chapters 2 and 3. But there have been many deviations
from the ideals expressed in these dominant perspectives.
Where it was stated that the media could be used for development purposes, in reality only radio to any substantial extent came to be used with such aims in mind. Newspaper and television content has been dominated by other
influences.

Newspapers

The dominant philosophy of development explicitly
presumed that the press would be privately owned with
little or no interference from the government. This
Western tradition of long standing is implicit in the
hallowed principle of "freedom of the press." In a development perspective, however, the drawbacks are obvious.
Since the chief purpose of a privately owned press is to
produce a profit for the owners, development subjects are
taken up only if they are considered profitable. The target group for newspapers is, quite naturally, people who

are literate. These groups are better educated than the
majority; most of them live in urban areas, and on the
whole they enjoy better living conditions than the majority. Consequently, they also have other interests and
other aspirations.

The content of newspapers reflects this audience. It
has to reflect it for newspapers to survive. Coverage of
development problems has been only slight and sporadic.
To the extent that such issues were taken up they were
looked at from the perspective of these target groups, the
already "modernized."

Although the situation for television is a bit different, there are similarities. Many countries did not
have television systems in the 1960s. Countries that invested in television, and many did, soon discovered how
expensive a medium it was, if that was not already evident
before. One hour of even the most rudimentary production,
with someone talking into a microphone, would cost on the
order of $1,000. For more complex programs the costs rose
steeply. But as soon as a television network had been set
up and transmission started, there was pressure for more
programming from those who had bought receiving sets.
Needless to say, these were the same groups that we have
identified above: the already better-off residents of urban areas.

Caught in such a situation, the broadcasting organizations in developing countries turned to importing foreign material. Katz (1973) and Katz and Wedell (1977)
describe this dilemma and estimate that one segment of an
American TV series of one hour would cost from about $250
to $400. Even considering a cost of subtitling, this is
still a very low expense for such action-oriented programs.
Often, this is also the kind of material that the groups
possessing TV sets say they want to watch. American films
shown at local movie theaters had already paved the way.
By importing such programs two nails are hit with one blow
of the hammer: popular programs at low costs. In countries where the television system was dependent on advertising revenues, high viewing figures were of course essential, and that meant a heavier reliance on popular imported series.

In Chapter 6 it is shown that this was something
peculiar not to a few countries only but was an overall
pattern in the world. Suffice it to say here that neither
television nor the "free press" lived up to the faith expressed in them.

Indeed, the cultural values spread through these
channels were often opposite to the development aims of
the majority of the people. The Western/American culture
was given a lot of time and space, while the indigenous
cultural expressions of the country were given very lim-

ited coverage. The creation of nation-ness, so stressed
by development theorists, benefited little from any of the
media, particularly television, which instead promoted the
values of Western industrialized societies.
Radio is the medium used most extensively for development purposes. Before continuing our discussion, some
of its particular uses should be made clear.

A Closer Look at Radio
Cost has been an important factor in making radio the
medium that has been most development oriented in both
content and in its ability to reach audiences in rural
areas. Production and transmission costs are comparatively low. In making a distinction between *Big Media* (television, sound films, computer assisted instruction) and
Little Media (radio, film strips), Schramm (1977) makes
the rough estimate that the per unit costs for the latter
are about one-fifth the costs involved in using the former.
Radio has been used in various different ways.
McAnany (1973) identifies five main forms of usage:

1. Open broadcasting. The typical pattern in most
developing nations is that only a small portion of the
total radio content--often under 10 percent--is devoted
to educational programs. The areas covered are agriculture and health, women's home programs, literacy classes,
etc. These programs are repeated two or three times
weekly, and in different languages where necessary. The
situation is different in various parts of the world but
the general pattern is the same.
2. Instructional radio. Radio is used as part of
the formal school system. Every school or classroom has a
receiver and the students listen to broadcasts as part of
their curricular training.
3. Radio rural forums. Farmers get together weekly
to listen to agricultural information and then discuss the
content. Often the discussion leads up to some kind of
action or decision related to the subject.
4. Radio schools. One of the most comprehensive
strategies for using radio in rural development was started in the small town of Sutatenza, Colombia, 25 years ago
by a parish priest. A national organization, Acción
Cultural Popular (ACPO), was formed and has transmitted
what is called "fundamental integral education" for some
years over the radio. This includes not only reading,
writing, and cognitive skills, but also a deepening of the
sense of dignity and worth of the farmer--the creation of
a "new man." Acción Cultural Popular's success over the
years seems to have been considerable, according to evaluative studies. Other radio schools have also been arranged, particularly in Latin America.

5. Radio and animation. The animation strategy is a method that promotes a dialogue in which community members participate in defining their development problems. It also includes working out ways to mobilize people to take common action to overcome these problems. The technique grew out of a French tradition of group dynamics that was applied to development strategies in the early 1960s. It has been of some importance in Latin America and West Africa.

A Lack of Evaluation

As can be seen from the description above, the radio-mediated activities include both formal and nonformal education. They have been aimed at adults and younger groups. But what have been the real outcomes? The most nearly correct answer, unfortunately, is that we do not exactly know. Very few studies have been carried out to evaluate the effects of information transmitted by the mass media. This is true not only for radio, but for other media used to carry development information as well. We know particularly little about the role of information via mass media in national development. Our knowledge is somewhat better for communication and changes in the village, but here too, it is difficult to use findings from research to make definite assessments as to the outcomes.

Now, why this lack of evaluative studies? There are several reasons. First of all, there is no real tradition of allocating resources to this aspect of planned communication activities. It is still more common to use input figures as indicators of the effects of a campaign.

Second, evaluations of interventions may be very risky. It is easier to *talk* about the advantageous outcomes than to run the risk of facing figures that show the real results are far from what was desired and expected.

A third and final reason is that it is difficult to evaluate information campaigns. Better nutrition serves as an example. Suppose the aim is to improve the nutritional status of the population of a particular village. A campaign tries to convey knowledge about the necessity of giving children milk, of boiling water, and of the composition of a healthful daily diet. The campaign also encourages people to go to the health clinic as soon as they notice any signs of malnutrition in themselves or, especially, in their infants. The typical campaign goes on for about two months. Its major components are information released by home visits of nurses, leaflets, posters at the health center, some meetings at the community development office, or perhaps even some spot announcements over the radio and in newspapers.

An evaluation should answer the question: Did the information activities really improve the nutritional status

of the population in the village? From a scientific point
of view it is difficult to give a simple answer to such a
question. People may come more frequently to the clinic,
but how do we know that this is a consequence of the campaign? It may only reflect an extreme scarcity of food
supplies, that people are actually worse off than before.
And what do measures of knowledge mean in a context
like this? People may respond that they now know how to
boil water and understand its importance, and that they
likewise have learned the basics of a balanced diet. But
does this result in improved nutritional status? No, not
in itself. It may be a step toward it, but this is not at
all certain. The only measure that could really be relied
on would be medical checkups and observations of how people actually behave in their homes. Have they made any
changes in the composition of their diet?

These are some of the main questions that have to be
taken up in evaluations of this kind. Still, they leave a
lot of other questions open. Did the campaign itself
bring about the changes, or did other more influential
things happen at the same time? Maybe the mere fact that
some newcomers to the village went around asking strange
questions produced the whole effect. The methodological
problems are great and, of course, greater in contexts
where even the drawing of a random sample may sometimes be
impossible. This clearly limits the possibilities of gen-
eralizing results to other areas and other issues.

Extending the School: The Case of El Salvador

Before presenting more overall conclusions on the
effects of educational activities by means of radio and
other media, a few words should also be said about use of
the media in the school setting. This reflects a plan for
teaching more students without training a larger number of
qualified teachers. The media are used to compensate for
the lack of teachers. Radio is not the only medium to
enter the classroom. Indeed, in coming years, television
rather than radio seems to be the medium that will be
used.

Among the countries that have introduced television
for instructional purposes in the school are Niger,
American Samoa, Mexico, and the Ivory Coast of Africa.
But the country that probably has made the largest educational reform using television in its curriculum is El
Salvador. In any case, the work undertaken there has been
most extensively documented. Stanford University was
given the task of following the introduction of television
over several years and evaluating the results--an excep-
tion from the general rule of a lack of thorough evaluations. Mayo, Hornik, and McAnany (eds., 1976) describe
the project and its findings in a summarizing book.

The problem in El Salvador was that although the law required all children to attend primary school, in practice only one child in seven who began school ever was graduated from the 6th grade. The high dropout and repeater rates stemmed from shortcomings in the rural areas, as well as from the grading and promotion policies applied throughout the system. Two-thirds of all rural schools did not offer six primary grades, and 60 percent of them had only one room and one teacher.

Another factor contributing to the high attrition rate among students was the inappropriateness of the curriculum, which was based on the humanistic values of nineteenth century European education and provided little practical guidance to teachers. Finally, there was little coordination between the curriculum and real life employment opportunities in the country. The curriculum was tailored to the needs of an elite minority of students destined for the university.

To remedy the numerous problems that this antiquated school system had created over the years, a 5-year Educational Reform plan was set forth in 1968. This involved several components, including reorganization of the Ministry of Education and curriculum revision. Of particular interest here is that all tuition in grades 7 to 9 was eliminated, and a new instructional television system for these grades was installed.

In 1973 the enrollment in grades 7, 8, and 9 had increased from about 20,000 to 65,000, so that matriculation was elevated to 34 percent of the 13-year-old to 15-year-old population. The large increase also resulted in a shift in the social background of students, with many pupils from poorer and rural homes registering for the first time.

Test results revealed a clear trend. Learning gains were significantly greater in the classes that relied fully on Instructional Television (ITV) than in classes where all parts of the educational reform, except ITV, had been introduced. Learning data were supplemented by periodic surveys of student attitudes and aspirations. A majority of students was favorable toward ITV throughout the 4 years in which attitudes were surveyed. However, high initial enthusiasm declined somewhat as students progressed from the 7th through 9th grades.

On the cost side too, the reform produced good results. It seems likely that the reform without ITV would not have been sufficient to attain the learning quality that was reached with ITV, but such conclusions must be somewhat speculative, since no information could be gathered on alternative instructional systems. However unlikely, the possibilities cannot be excluded that an investment in some other technology, or in such things as

additional teacher training, higher salaries, and better
classroom resources would have been as effective as ITV.
     Having characterized some specific uses of communica-
tion for development, our next step is to make a more general analysis. This will be done under two headings: (1)
use of the media in the school, and (2) use of the media
outside the school. The discussion will take up the two
levels of development that were put under our critical eye
in Chapters 2 and 3: development of the nation and development at the village level.

USE OF THE MEDIA IN THE SCHOOL

     Because of the lack of technical equipment, trained
personnel, and other material resources, the media have
not been widely used in the classroom. Consequently, not
many young people have been educated through media use.
At least not many when the count is compared to population
figures in the Third World.
     The case of El Salvador is in many ways unique, and
one of the conclusions to be drawn from this example is
that many similar prerequisites would have to be at hand
in order to increase the number of students and the quality of what is being taught.
     For example, no language problem is present in El
Salvador; Spanish is the first language for everyone. It
is a small, relatively homogeneous country with a topog-
raphy that permits television signals to reach its various
parts. This makes the use of an instructional television
system less costly than in many other countries. Moreover, El Salvador received very favorable financial aid
from abroad to cover many of the fixed costs of the project (production studios, hardware). Foreign advisors were
kept under stricter control than in many other countries;
unless they corresponded to needs defined by the Salvadorean Ministry of Education, they were not requested.
(In other countries, for example, the foreign influence
grew to such magnitude that projects were more or less
discontinued once the advisors had left the country.) To
all these circumstances came the fact that the person responsible for the reform and its implementation had the
interest, knowledge, and ability to pull the project
through all the administrative and bureaucratic bottle-
necks that always exist in complex organizations.
     The cost comparisons in El Salvador showed favorable
results. Although it could not be definitely proved that
the choice of television was the best way to attain greater attendance and better learning, this was the conclusion
drawn by several observers. Elsewhere, however, few cost
comparisons involving the media have been carried out, and
the discussion of costs seems to be filled with confusion

and biases that make generalizations difficult. This is
an area for further research, and this point is included
in the list of relevant research topics in Chapter 9.

The problem with many cost comparisons is that different teaching activities strive towards different objectives, but this it not taken into account when putting
their costs side by side. Some forms of teaching aim only
to spread knowledge of a very specific, skill-related
kind, while others have more complex and long-term objectives. The school generally wants to transmit values and
behaviors basic to their society. It wants its students
to internalize the democratic values the nation recognizes
as its own.

When comparing different teaching situations (with or
without the new media involved), the aims of each must be
made clear. The situations may be different, and in such
cases it is not correct merely to compare the costs for
teaching the specific skills. The grounds for comparisons
have to be made explicit. This is seldom done, however,
and hence it is difficult to assess to what extent the use
of the media has been worth the investment.

Carnoy and Levin (1975, p. 386) comment upon the
quality of studies within this problem area. They make
the general statement that evaluations of media for instructional purposes show a consistent tendency to favor
the new technology, which is given what they call "the
benefit of the doubt." When costs for two alternative
teaching methods are difficult to estimate, the expendi-
tures for the one favoring the use of a new technology are
systematically underestimated. The authors point out that
such a result is the outcome of a situation where evaluators have close contacts with the funding agencies supporting such projects: "often their evaluations have been
sponsored directly by the agencies and personnel who have
planned, funded, and implemented the particular educational technology that is being reviewed."

In a more general sense this refers to the "first
law" Wilson (1973, p. 138) set forth regarding evaluation
of public policy: "All policy interventions in social
problems produce the intended effect--*if* the research is
carried out by those implementing the policy, or their
friends."

Much of the evaluation of instructional technology
has been carried out in such a manner. It is not that
evaluators are overtly partisan but in their examination
of system costs (and effectiveness) they tend to have an
implicitly favorable attitude toward the technology. This
causes them to deal with the potential sources for error
in such a way as to understate the true costs of the technology system.

A Link between Improved Education and Development?
    In drawing our conclusions as to classroom use of the
media, the first point is that the media have been used
to only a limited extent. Where substantial investments
in such systems have been made, the outcomes have had some
elements of success. This has to be interpreted in a
limited sense, though: those who have attended have
learned the contents better.
    But the crucial matter to consider is to what extent
improved education with the help of the new media led to
the improved living standards that the dominant model in
communication promised.
    The conclusion to be drawn from 20 years of experi-
ence is this: even if a country succeeds in increasing the
educational level of its inhabitants, there is nothing
that says this will automatically lead to a way out of the
state of underdevelopment. As Carnoy (1974, p. 51)
states:

> Implicit in this spread of formal schooling is a
> fundamental belief in the ability of capitalism to
> provide everyone with work through the market, and in
> the ability of schooling to turn traditional, unpro-
> ductive human beings into productive elements in
> capitalist development. Neither of these premises
> seems to hold empirically.

    The example from El Salvador can again be used to
illustrate these mechanisms. El Salvador relies on private enterprise to undertake industrialization and to increase commercialization of the agricultural sector. The
government provides the necessary infrastructure for industry. It also encourages the most modern methods in
business management and industrial production.
    The assumption implicit in the development model is
that the modern sector of the economy will progressively
expand to absorb the population into areas of higher
productivity than now exist in the traditional sector. In
this way, eventually El Salvador will be a modern country
in the Western sense. One of the main hopes and aims is
to attract foreign investment by offering cheap labor for
the assembly or manufacture of goods for export to advanced countries.
    Through its educational reform El Salvador hoped to
prepare young people for technical jobs in industry and
agriculture. But by 1972 there were relatively few technical jobs for students graduating from the 9th grade. A
large proportion of the students therefore wanted to continue on to university education instead of entering the
job market. If economic expansion (in other words, investments by domestic and foreign capital) fails to match

the large increase in school enrollments, students will be
forced to reconsider the kind of middle-level jobs they
currently refuse as unsuitable. If the number of job opportunities does not increase, all but the most menial
positions may require a 9th-grade education.

It does not seem that foreign investors have become
more inclined to transfer capital to El Salvador since the
educational reform was initiated. The social benefits of
the reform are consequently disappointing. Surely there
may be such individual improvements as increased self-
confidence, innovativeness, and creativity. But the pay-
off for society as a whole is meager, and the future pros-
pects for the country do not alter this impression.

The government also seems to be well aware of this.
In drafting the second 5-year Educational Reform plan
(1973-1977), Salvadorean planners turned their attention
to the needs of other groups and the adult population at
large. According to observers at a conference at Stanford
University (Mayo, ed. 1976, p. 112), Salvadorean planners
recognize that "schooling alone would never solve deeply
rooted economic problems, and that modern technology is no
substitute for basic political and social reform."

Hence, the faith expressed in what the media could
accomplish by acting as teachers inside the school system
was not well founded. The basic assumptions were much too
simplified, and the automatic link assumed to exist between improved teaching and benefits to society in the
form of national and local progress turned out not to be
there.

USE OF THE MEDIA OUTSIDE THE SCHOOL
Leaving the classroom, we turn to consider various
teaching efforts outside the conventional school setting.
Adult education programs form one essential part of these
activities but the media have also been directed toward
younger age groups.

In many countries the Ministry of Education or some
special branch outside the ministry has been responsible
for the organization of these activities.

But many other governmental organizations, private
nonprofit or profit-making, have also engaged in information activities. Agriculture, health, nutrition, family
planning, and community development seem to be the subjects covered most extensively. They are still given high
priority today.

A special kind of teaching is represented in the *campaign*, a concentrated activity that goes on for a limited
time and deals with a clearly defined topic. A mixture of
media is generally used. The campaign approach has been

used in most countries, but the resources allocated have
varied tremendously.

Although there are great differences in the planning,
execution, and outcomes of educational efforts of this
kind, they have certain common features in their use.
These can be brought together in four broad points:

1. *Overoptimism about information.* As in many industrialized nations, information has been used in the
developing countries as a panacea for problems of the most
varying kinds. Some of the problems attacked have been of
an informational nature, while in just as many other instances the problem at hand has been of another character,
and information activities, no matter how cleverly designed and carried out, have had little to do with the
solution of the problem. On this ground alone many campaigns have failed and resources have been wasted.

2. *Information alone.* In many development efforts
where information has been used, communication activities
alone have been relied on to provide the impetus for
change. Findings from research show that communication
has to be coupled with other efforts in order to bring
about genuine change (Brown and Kearl 1967, p. 25):

> Skillful communication can change a peasant's per-
> ceptions of his situation, but it cannot, *acting
> alone* [my emphasis], change that situation very much.
> It can help a backward farmer to see opportunities
> he ignores, but if few opportunities exist, informa-
> tion will not create them.

This "information alone" approach has been most common, and not until much later has the idea of integrated
development, whereby not one but several things are
changed at the same time, been accepted.

3. *Lack of coordination.* Another aspect of the education campaigns in societies with free enterprise economies is that when they have been carried out, they have
not been coordinated systematically. They have also
lacked an overall common objective. This is different
from campaigns undertaken in planned economies; some of
their approaches to communication will be discussed in the
next chapter. But on the capitalist road to development
there are so many actors in the development arena that
many of their activities overlap, collide in time, and
sometimes carry conflicting messages.

For example, in recent years private companies have
launched campaigns centered around their own products, but
with a "twist" of social progress. One such case is the
promotion of bottle-feeding of supplementary milk instead
of breast-feeding. At the same time doctors and nurses

have urged just the opposite: "Do not bottle-feed. It
gives the child infections. Breast-feed instead!" Whom
is the mother to believe?
     Likewise we have many examples where communication
activities have not been well synchronized. Several campaigns may be competing for the citizen's attention at one
time, only to be succeeded by a period of absolute lull.
Farmers, workers, housewives have had little chance to
benefit from any of the competing messages.
     4. *Reliance on Western models for information dis-
semination.* When it became widely accepted that the mass
media and communication should be applied in a systematic
way to reach development aims, the practical techniques of
spreading the information had to be taken from somewhere.
Since the desired new media were developed in the West and
had been used there for several years, it was natural to
borrow "professional information thinking" that had been
elaborated there, as well.
     This transfer of Western models for information dis-
semination was in many ways unfortunate, however. An important part of the criticism raised against the dominant
approach to communication pivots on this fact. The guidelines that came to be followed were the principles for
commercial campaigns carried out in Europe and the United
States. The problems of improving nutrition, public
health, and agricultural practices were reduced to questions of media choice, design of posters and pamphlets,
and formulating catchy slogans. This is another reason
why many campaigns failed. People greeted the new methods
of persuasion with great skepticism: the simple arguments
on posters and leaflets or the pictures of "successful
family" bore little resemblance to their own situations
and problems.
     Another aspect is that this commercial approach to
communication tended to concentrate on the Western mass
media. Traditional channels of communication, patron-
izingly referred to as "folk media," were bypassed. Introducing new ideas by means of "alien" media was another
way of saying that the old, established communication
structure was outdated, "unmodern," and backward. No
trust in the new authorities could be created by relying
so heavily on the new media in this Western way.
     These questions are not unimportant. But the most
important question concerning a campaign is first of all
whether it should be carried out at all. This issue
should have been given much greater attention. Such inquiry would have found that many of the problems approached were of such a nature that communication activities had little to do with their solutions.
     More could be said about all the difficulties that
were encountered when relying on these Western ways of

distributing information but such failures are documented
in the several case studies that have been reported. An
interesting discussion of some particular problems can be
found in Fuglesang (1973).
    Another point should be made, however. The Western
way of disseminating information by means of the mass
media is clearly a one-way process. Most of the messages
contain rules, orders, or recommendations for people to
behave or think in certain ways. But for development to
occur, participation by the people is an important prerequisite. At least it is necessary for getting proposed
changes accepted and implemented on a large scale. This
was also recognized in the dominant communication model.
    One-way information flows through the mass media did
not stimulate such participation, however. The messages
put out were more or less authoritarian commands. They
neither stimulated discussion nor gave suggestions as to
how people's active involvement in community affairs could
be increased. It is conceivable that such authoritarian
modes of communication may instead have driven people away
from what must be considered society's inherent interest
in exerting influence over its living conditions.

SUCCESS OR FAILURE?
    The critique that was expressed against the dominant
communication model in its application at the national and
local levels made it clear that the model had serious limitations. It failed to recognize that the major obstacles
to development lay in the relationships between poor and
rich countries. Consequently, no matter how successful
the communication activities, they could not break the
state of underdevelopment.
    In judging the use of the media with this general
picture kept in mind, we realize the outcomes are mixed.
In the context of the school, some efforts seem to have
been successful, although there are examples also of the
opposite. But even these cases of success have not automatically led to any substantially improved living conditions. With regard to this overall objective, the programs have not been nearly as successful and many of them
have actually failed.
    At the local level the experience has been similar.
Kincaid, Park, Chung, and Lee (1975) describe one well-
known case of success that sometimes has been called "the
miracle of Oryu Li" (after the village in Korea). The
Planned Parenthood Federation of Korea organized women's
clubs in several villages to disseminate the idea of family planning through interpersonal contacts and local
opinion leadership. In Oryu Li the project achieved remarkable success, not only in lowered birth rates, but

above all in a general improvement of the village. Job
opportunities were created, smaller educational programs
were created, and the fertility of the land was improved.
Perhaps the most important outcome was that it not only
became accepted that women could openly practice family
planning, but it was granted that women had *rights* in society too.

Unfortunately, the lessons of this example are difficult to generalize into a program for bringing about
changes at the village level. Were this not so, all the
other villages which were failures might simply have
adopted the Oryu Li way. Rather, a number of critical
events helped Oryu Li; these ranged from a remarkable village woman leader to visits from the provincial governor.

Thus, the overall record of use of the media for educational purposes is hardly one of many success stories.
As noted earlier, use of the media in these contexts was
guided by the model of innovation diffusion (discussed in
Chapter 3). Generally speaking, the hopes attached to the
"extension" model, applied with some success in North
America, were not fulfilled in the developing countries.

In a thorough examination of the record after some
15 years' empirical experience, Rogers, Eveland, and Bean
(1976) claim that the model was really not well suited to
the agricultural field. The adaptation of the model to
the area of family planning worked somewhat better. Their
conclusion is that the extension model has had little success, the main reason being that it paid too little attention to providing motivation for adopting innovations.

But this is only part of the story. A more important
explanation is the fact that only a few in the "target
group" could respond by adopting. Only those who possessed the necessary resources could invest in the machinery or new seeds and fertilizers that were proposed.
These were also the groups that reaped benefit from the
Western development philosophy upon which this approach
rests. Once again, the blindness of the dominant model of
development to societal and sociological factors thwarted
many efforts made in the field.

Another explanation for the low degree of success is
that people chose not to adopt because they were actually
better off by not doing so. Their skepticism against the
proinnovation policy that authorities and agents advocated
was sound.

ADDITIONAL READINGS:

Spain, P. L.; Jamison, D. T.; and McAnany, E. G., 1977,
    "Radio for Education and Development: Case Studies."

A document of the Education Department of the World Bank.

Mayo, J. K., and Spain, P. L., 1977, *Communication Policy Planning for Education and Development*, Conference Report. Stanford, Calif.: Institute for Communication Research, Stanford University.

5

Flows between Countries

Just as the discussion in the previous chapters has shown that all the hopes for domestic development attached to the media have not been realized, the same failures can be registered in the international arena. The media did not come to be carriers of the cultural *exchange* seen as desirable; instead, they came to be powerful instruments for cultural *domination*.

PRINCIPLE OF "FREE FLOW" OF INFORMATION

For almost 30 years the international flows of information have followed the basic doctrine that messages should be allowed to travel freely, independent of national barriers. Historically the roots of this principle go back to the end of World War II. The people of Europe and other parts of the world had for a long time lived under great strain. In the field of communication, propaganda and censorship were the rule of the day.

So when the United States--in the role of liberator--proclaimed the principle of a "free flow" of information between countries as a cornerstone of its policy, the idea won great response. The concept of freedom quite naturally had great attraction.

Although altruistic motives were held forth, other factors may have been even more important. Nordenstreng and Varis (1975) and Schiller (1976a) point out economic motives. The British and French empires had long controlled large sectors of world commerce, and the rapidly expanding United States had not been able to increase its spheres of interest quickly enough. One area in which the United States had but little influence was the international communication network. At this time the British agency Reuters was the dominant international news distributor. Control of the international flow of news and information was recognized as an essential prerequisite

to being able to establish and maintain worldwide commercial and military systems.

The war gave the United States an opportunity to alter the status quo. The British and French news agencies
had run into financial difficulties, and the American news
agencies Associated Press (AP) and United Press International (UPI) came onto the international news scene with
strong support from both the United States' business world
and government. Business groups in North America clearly
recognized the great importance of the news/information
function for incorporating new parts of the world as tar-
gets for trade and investments.

Such economic motives were not, however, made explicit to the American public or the world. Instead, a political campaign was launched by the press associations,
publishing companies, and private industry to make the
principle of free flow of information nationally and
internationally accepted. This campaign also used the
opportunity to foment suspicion of countries that had chosen social systems other than the North American one,
principally the Soviet Union and members of the "Eastern
bloc."

The "free flow" doctrine won wide acceptance in the
United States even before the war ended. The next step
was to get it internationally accepted. This could be
done in UNESCO as early as 1946, and it proved to be no
real difficulty since the United Nations was a quite different organization than it is today. The United States
had a substantially greater influence at that time.

This is also the background to the formulation of
Article 19 in the Universal Declaration of Human Rights
adopted in 1948 concerning the individual's right to seek,
receive, and impart information. Other documents, including the Constitution of UNESCO, expressed the same basic
idea. The United States drew up the guidelines, received
support from its allies in other parts of the world, and
eventually the support of the socialist countries as well.

The Principle at Work

Looking back at almost 30 years of experience with
the free flow principle, we find the same conclusion can
be drawn as for the dominant communication model formulated in the early 1960s: the outcome does not match up
with the benefits that were promised. On the contrary,
many signs tell us that something has definitely gone
wrong. A free and equal exchange of information between
countries has never come to be. Instead a clear one-way
flow has emerged, and the problems emanating from this
have been the topic of several conferences during the past
decade.

The empirically based critique presented by the developing countries concerns the total flow of information in the world. Specifically, the points of criticism deal with how different media are controlled and with the content that fills them.

News agencies. Somavia (1976) is one of the most outspoken critics of the news agency system. First of all, he uses the term *transnational enterprises* rather than international enterprises to describe the agencies, the most important of which in the Third World are Associated Press, United Press International, and Agence France-Presse. Transnational implies that ownership and control remain totally in the hands of the interests in one country, the home country of the enterprise.

Under the cover of the principle of free flow of information, these news agencies have obtained a certain form of independence and they have been able to transmit their views of events and news freely in less-developed countries. But their independence is only apparent. Their activities are interlinked with other parts of the transnational system of which they themselves are an integral part. Quite obviously, they have an interest in seeing to it that the existing order, which gives transnational corporations their powerful position, prevails and is not threatened.

Consequently, this structural situation also influences the news reporting that these agencies almost monopolize. The criteria used for selecting news are based on the political and economic interests of the transnational system and the countries in which the agencies have their owners. This means that information that shows the existing system works well is given priority over events that imply criticism. Political movements are classified in accordance with their potential threat to the system. Leaders who want to bring about fundamental changes in the political, social, and economic conditions in a country are labeled "extremists," "guerrillas," or the equivalent, while those who work for the system are characterized as "legitimate," or "pragmatically oriented."

The enormous strength of the transnational news agencies also distorts the news in other respects. One obvious distortion lies in the fact that news from the Third World is presented to the rest of the world and interpreted in the light of the interests of the industrialized world and above all the United States. Examples of such reporting can be found in the coverage of various negotiations among developing countries in their efforts to increase their control over world market prices on raw materials. The OPEC-conferences of the 1970s are striking examples, but there are many more, not all as widely covered.

The developing countries have little or no way of making their own affairs clear to the rest of the world. There are many national news agencies in Africa, Asia, and Latin America but they have little chance of reaching beyond the national borders. The news that the rest of the world gets is seen through the eyes of alien observers.

Furthermore, this system hardly facilitates better communication among the developing countries themselves. In fact, the news about one African country that reaches the people in another African country has often gone through the international news agencies. The news that the reader in Botswana gets about Peru has probably passed through New York for compilation and editing.

This, of course, is a very unsatisfactory situation for countries in the underdeveloped world. It hinders a better understanding among nations in similar situations. Better information exchange among such countries might lead also to cooperation to combat conditions they face together. The present structural situation, however, makes joint initiatives difficult. Such a situation is naturally favorable to already powerful nations.

Hence, if there is to be a change in the information scene, it has to be brought about by the underdeveloped countries themselves.

Television. Many developing nations invest much money in building television systems. The motives for this may differ, but, whatever the reason, television is often given high priority. One objective seems to be present in most countries: that of promoting the indigenous national culture and strengthening the feeling of "one people, one nation."

But when we survey the world television scene today, it seems very doubtful whether these hopes have been fulfilled to any large extent. Nordenstreng and Varis (1974) have made an inventory of television program contents in various parts of the world, and their results prove that many developing countries rely heavily on imported material with very little air time devoted to domestically produced programs. In such cases the idea of using the medium for creating or supporting local and national cultures has lost all meaning.

According to the figures presented in this UNESCO report there are wide variations in the ratio between foreign and domestic productions. Some general conclusions can be made, however. Four countries have a very small proportion of imports: the United States and China with less than 2 percent from abroad, and Japan and the Soviet Union with even less.

By contrast, about half the television programs in Latin America are of foreign origin. In Asia, aside from

China and Japan, two distinct groups exist. One group
imports one-third or less of its output, whereas the other
imports more than 50 percent. In the four African countries in the study (Ghana, Nigeria, Uganda, Zambia) on
average, imported material makes up roughly one-half the
output.

Looking at the international flows of programs, a
clear pattern can be seen. There are four major exporters
--the United States, Great Britain, France, and the
Federal Republic of Germany--with the United States by far
the most important source of television material. At the
time of the study (early 1970s), the United States, with
an annual export of 150,000 hours, sent abroad more than
triple the combined total of the other three countries.
Most of this export consisted of entertainment programs
but there was also a smaller portion of documentaries and
educational material.

The picture that emerges is distinct. The international flows of television programs go in one direction,
from the developed to the underdeveloped countries. American entertainment programs are well-known phenomena in
large parts of the world, and the characters in these series may be as popular in Thailand, Kenya, or Venezuela
as they are in the United States.

The reasons for this one-way traffic are several and
may differ somewhat from country to country. But some
underlying factors, touched upon in previous chapters, are
common to most nations. Once a country has committed itself to the new technology with all its heavy capital investment, a need is felt to make use of the equipment.
Pressure comes from the audience, who also have had capital
outlays for buying and installing a television set. These
are the literate, relatively well-educated, urban elites,
influential pressure groups in a developing nation.

Caught between these demands, the importation of
television programs has been often relied upon. Buying
from abroad means more hours over the air at a lesser cost
than producing the material domestically. Also, sales
representatives from the international divisions of producing companies in the United States, often connected to
film corporations in Hollywood, have offered favorable
financial terms (Varis 1973).

Other Communication Channels

Advertising. Imbalances in information flows and contents
are clear in other areas as well. Schiller (1976b) shows
that as the transnational corporations have increased
their markets over the world, they have also come to use
more advertising to put their products on the commercial
market. United States' dominance has increased rapidly in

this area, probably more than in any other communication
area (Schiller 1976b, p. 177): "Of the 25 largest agencies
in the world in 1975, 22 are U.S.-owned or closely associated with U.S. capital."

This picture is even more pronounced in developing
countries: American companies dominate the advertising
industry. This means that the whole system for selling
commercial products has been even further penetrated by
alien values. Since the advertising industry in the
United States is the most advanced in the world, this
probably also means that the efficiency of advertising in
the Third World has increased.

The transnational companies are part of a system that
promotes a life-style built on the individual possession
of consumer goods. Through advertising they have disseminated this style of life to countries all over the world.
But seen from the point of view of the welfare of the community as a whole, the pattern and standards of consumption that these companies try to impose on populations
around the world may very well represent a grave misallo-
cation of national resources (see also Evans 1972).

The interests of the advertising industry do not stop
at promotional activities for products and consumer goods,
however. Most, if not to say all, American advertising
agencies and their foreign affiliates are involved in
several other communication activities. They have financial interests in companies engaged in market research,
films, videotape production, publishing, and management
consulting. In this way the influence of the advertising
agencies is strengthened even further. Their central importance to the functioning of the capitalist transnational system is beyond any doubt.

Films, magazines, music, computers. Under the free flow
doctrine, the United States and other industrialized nations have also provided the world with other media products. One such area is films. The motion picture industry in Hollywood was the first in the world to begin production on a large scale, and the domestic market was so
large that several film companies could exist side by side.
On the global scene this resulted in an American predomi-
nance since production and distribution could benefit from
economies of scale (Boyd-Barrett 1977). Another motivating force behind this leading position in the world was
the domestic competition between film companies, which led
to a search for new or unpenetrated markets outside the
United States.

Guback (1969 and 1974) makes a detailed analysis of
the international film industry. Among other things, he
points to the fact that American capital in the business
is nowadays transferred abroad, and although the films are

made in other countries, the economic returns still go to
the American owner-groups.

To this catalogue of international media domination
must also be added the wide distribution of such North
American magazines and periodicals as *Newsweek*, *Time*,
Reader's Digest, and *Playboy*. The comics industry has
been extremely successful, Donald Duck being a well-known
character in many countries (see Dorfman and Mattelart
1975, for an analysis of the ideological contents of this
Walt Disney product).

Although almost no data are available, the worldwide
influence of American and British popular music also be-
longs to the picture. Neither the actual volume of imports in different parts of the world nor the effects
thereof have been investigated, but the general impression
is that by the "internationalization" of music, "the
American way" has reached incredibly large segments of
younger age-groups around the world. The effects of this
phenomenon relate not only to the music itself, but to the
life-style dictated by the sales agents who are experts in
packaging the music and the artists.

The industrialized countries also enjoy a strong position in the computer industry. The use of computers and
auxiliary technology is definitely a business with Western
origins. The United States, by far the most advanced
country in the computer field, has spread its influence to
almost all corners of the globe. Very little research has
been carried out concerning all the problems that developing countries face when using United States-owned computer
technology and services. The role of the transnational
companies has yet to be made clear so that we might fully
understand the implications of the one-way flow in this
rapidly expanding field.

FROM "FREE FLOW" TO "BALANCED FLOW"

Throughout this overview of the different media and
their international reach there emerges a consistent pattern. The media that cover the world are American and, to
a lesser extent, British, French, and German. This is
true of ownership, distribution, and organizational structure in almost all areas in the communication sector
(Tunstall 1977). With no exaggeration whatever, the term
media domination seems to describe the situation in the
world today quite correctly. The developing countries
have a weak mass media structure. The media that do exist
are filled with programs from the metropoles in which the
transnational companies operate and the program content
reflects the interests of these organizations.

The term *cultural domination* goes one step further.
The world media structure means that a majority of nations

are denied the chance to preserve and strengthen their own
cultures. Instead, the media serve as mediators of values
of a commercially oriented life-style with its roots in
the industrialized world.
Not until the 1970s have these questions been given
serious attention. Until that time it was assumed that
the free flow principle would bring benefits to all involved, but now the consequences of outside domination of
the mass media in a developing country are apparent and
cause great concern. The question has to be asked: What
chance does a new nation have to create and maintain a
national culture in a context in which media domination
leads to cultural domination, preventing local and national endeavors?
This has meant a questioning of the free flow. The
following is a quotation from a speech by Urho Kekkonen,
President of Finland, taken from the Proceedings of the
Symposium on the International Flow of Television Programs,
University of Tampere, Finland, May 21-23, 1973:

> The traditional Western concept of freedom, which
> states that the state's only obligation is to guaran-
> tee laissez-faire, has meant that society has allowed
> freedom of speech to be realized with the means at
> the disposal of each individual. In this way freedom
> of speech has in practice become the freedom of the
> well-to-do.
> In the world of communication it can be observed
> how problems of freedom of speech within one state
> are identical to those in the world community formed
> by different states. At an international level are
> to be found the ideals of free communication and
> their actual distorted execution for the rich on the
> one hand and the poor on the other. Globally the
> flow of information between states--not least the
> material pumped out by television--is to a very great
> extent a one-way, unbalanced traffic, and in no way
> possesses the depth and range which the principles of
> freedom of speech require.

During the 1970s, the free flow issue has been discussed at several meetings of the nonaligned countries,
which include a large number of developing countries.
There is wide agreement that something has to be done to
change the existing pattern of international flows of information. Varis (1976) has studied the proceedings of
several of these meetings, and the conclusion is that only
well-organized cooperation between nonaligned countries
can bring about a balanced and equitable distribution of
news and information to the peoples of the world.
To further underline the importance of such a new

orientation in the communication field, the concept of a
New International Information Order has been coined. It
should be regarded not as a particular order in itself,
but as an integral part of a New International Economic
Order, which is the overall objective.

Efforts to alter the international flows of information encounter tremendous problems since the flows are so
heavily intertwined with economic and political interests
in the world. Can only the element of *information* be
altered in a system in which all the parts are mutually
related and interdependent? The close links between information and economic relations has been strongly
stressed at meetings of the nonaligned countries in the
mid-1970s. Meanwhile, however, various efforts to improve
communication intrastructures within the context of existing political relationships have been made.

One such effort was the New Delhi Ministerial Conference of 1976, where it was decided to create a pool of
news from the national agencies of these countries.
Around fifty nations are currently taking part in this exchange of news items, which is channeled through TANJUG,
the national news agency in Yugoslavia. The role of
TANJUG is largely confined to administering the pool.
News items are collected and distributed to other members
without editorial changes.

The pool should be seen not as an alternative, but as
a complement, to the big four agencies--AP, UPI, Reuters,
and AFP. Its main function is to give the developing
countries better information about each other. In the
common terminology where *south* stands for developing nations and *north* for the industrialized nations, the prime
aim of the pool is to increase the south-south dialogue.
But it also has some spillover effects that contribute to
a south-north exchange of information.

An alternative news channel which focuses on the
north-south flow is Inter-Press Service (IPS), established
in 1964 by a cooperative of Latin American journalists.
It is now represented in fifty countries. But neither
does IPS pose a real alternative to the Big Four. Instead,
IPS tries to concentrate on other kinds of news items:
people's liberation, popular movements within countries,
women's problems. Unable to compete in speed with the
others, IPS offers alternative news content.

"FREE AND BALANCED FLOW"
In the face of increasing demands from the Third
World, UNESCO has had to respond. A concept that has been
suggested to replace the free flow principle is the "free
and balanced" flow principle. But, for this change in
terminology, UNESCO has been strongly attacked by organi-

zations seeking to preserve the existing structure of information distribution. Naturally, among these are the
large news agencies and other supporters of the transnational enterprise system. Another response on the part of
UNESCO was the appointment of a special commission at the
1976 General Conference in Nairobi, the Commission for the
Study of Communication Problems. The commission was given
a mandate (UNESCO 1978, pp. 14-15):

> to study the current situation in the fields of com-
> munication and information and to identify problems
> which call for fresh action
> --to pay particular attention to problems relating to
> the free and balanced flow of information in the
> world ...
> --to analyse communication problems, in their dif-
> ferent aspects, within the perspective of the
> establishment of a new international economic
> order ...
> --to define the role which communication might play
> in making public opinion aware of the major prob-
> lems besetting the world ...

The establishing of the commission should not only be
seen as a concession to the demands from the developing
world, although the Nairobi conference was the scene of a
heated discussion concerning a proposal on a declaration
of the responsibilities of the mass media for strengthening peace by combating war propaganda, racialism, and
apartheid. The debate came to an open conflict between
opposing political ideologies and nations. A draft proposal was supported by the developing countries but in
order to avoid antagonistic confrontation and yet at the
same time pay deference to the Third World, UNESCO chose
to refer the problems to a special commission.

The draft proposal was not left to the commission,
however. It was rewritten and finally adopted at the
general conference in Paris in 1978. By this time it had
been changed substantially and was now clearly a compro-
mise. The south had moderated its demands in return for
promises from the north of financial assistance in the
building of mass media infrastructures in the Third World.

It is also important to note that the final version
of the adopted declaration does not use the concept "free
and balanced flow" that UNESCO had earlier accepted.
Instead, the concept used in Article I is "a free flow and
a wider and better balanced dissemination of information."
Likewise, the new conditions to be created in the field of
information are described as "a new, more just and more
effective world information and communication order" (Pre-
amble 16).

These changes in terminology are not unimportant. On the contrary, they indicate that the West has managed to render the calls for change from many developing nations less threatening to its own position. The nonaligned movement, no longer united, has not succeeded in carrying through into action at the international level its earlier, commonly agreed upon demands. This is a step backward, but so far not of crucial size. Political struggle (which is how these efforts should be seen) is always a question of gaining experience and finding the right strategy.

SUGGESTIONS FOR A NEW ORDER

The implementation of a New International Information Order requires changes on many levels. The political aspects have already been touched upon. Regional cooperation in the exchange of news has been mentioned, and the practical work has gone the furthest in this area. Many more small steps have been taken, however. Technology poses a problem for many developing countries. They do not have the facilities and they often lack money to get them. New, "small" technology, however, may make it easier to transmit news without the conventional hardware. A concrete example is a portable, relatively inexpensive unit which transforms written text into signals which are then transmitted at high speed over the regular telephone system. A similar unit decodes the message into written text. In such a way the conventional telex system with all its drawbacks can be circumnavigated. This procedure may be one small step toward a new order.

Other factors that have been discussed concern the possibilities of establishing ethical codes for the media on a worldwide basis. But such actions seem to be fraught with difficulties, particularly with respect to how these rules should be formulated and how violations should be penalized. What sanctions should an International Press Council or an International Press Ombudsman be able to impose? The possibilities of finding some meaningful organization and ethical norms are small. So, although such a system might function well within some nations, the ideas cannot be translated to regulate the relations between nations.

Furthermore, the concept of what constitutes news should be critically examined. The kinds of events in the Third World that are given coverage in the media in developed countries paint a fragmentary, incomplete, and even false picture of what is happening in those nations. This is, of course, not a problem peculiar to the developing part of the world. It is much more general.

The usual argument in defense of the present way of selecting and presenting news events is that the media (in

the West) are selling a product on a commercial market,
and that they must give customers what they want. Such
an argument is no defense for media that are not selling a
product, however. Take, for example, broadcasting systems
such as the British Broadcasting Company (BBC) and the
Swedish Broadcasting Company (SBC). These do not differ
markedly from the pattern in the commercial media. And,
even if it may be true that it is easier to sell a product
that concentrates on dramatic events, why is this so? The
reader is accustomed to certain contents, a certain style
of presentation, but claiming that this is the immutable
and eternal taste of the consumer reveals a low regard for
the potential of the reader, listener, or viewer. Habits
and expectations can change if ways to alternatives are
shown. It is up to the media to show such new ways of
news coverage in their reporting from the developing countries, too. The noncommercial media are best equipped to
open up such roads, and they could exert pressure on the
other media to change their styles, too.

This raises the problem of journalism training around
the world. A new order requires a new role for journalists. Their loyalties should be with the public, not with
the owners of the media. Journalism training in many
Third World countries seems to need several changes to
meet the ideas that are implicit in a new information order. Western dominance has extended also to this arena,
and indigenous professional values have to be elaborated
in each country in order to replace or modify the Western
professional codes that so long have prevailed.

Another aspect of the prerequisites for better reporting between countries is that journalists are given
access to information sources and protection in law.
Otherwise, there is little point in training and sending
correspondents abroad. Efforts have also been made to
formulate such working conditions for journalists, the
most recent and important of these being the Helsinki
Agreement of 1975. What complicates the picture, however,
is the widespread misuse of the journalistic profession
for political interference in the internal affairs of other countries. See, for example, Petrusenko (1978).

In this list of the various measures and reforms
needed to achieve a new order, some technological aspects
should also be mentioned:

1. Rules should be formulated for the equitable use
of satellites. This whole area is very unclear, and in
light of the new technologies, available international
principles must be arrived at. Otherwise, the whole idea
of a more equitable information order will fail. One such
agreement that has been reached concerns the problem posed
by direct transmission via satellites, that is, a country

broadcasts directly into the television sets of citizens of another nation without any relaying ground station. When brought before the United Nations General Assembly, the proposition of prior consent from the receiving country was supported by a vote of 102 to 1. The sole opposing vote was cast by the United States.

2. The spectrum of radio frequencies is a finite asset, which must be shared much more equitably than it is today. The World Radio Administrative Conference, held in 1979, once again showed that the power structure that rules the world also rules the allocation of frequencies. The industrialized countries together control the best parts of the electromagnetic spectrum.

RIGHT TO COMMUNICATE

Parallel to, and sometimes crossing, the paths toward a New International Information Order is a discussion revolving around another concept: the "right to communicate." By the mid 1970s this discussion had also reached UNESCO levels.

The point of departure for this discussion has been Article 19 in the Universal Declaration of Human Rights of 1948: "Everyone has the right to freedom of opinion and expression; this right includes freedom to hold opinions without interference and to seek, receive, and impart information and ideas through any media and regardless of frontiers." But to communicate is something much more than this, according to the proponents of the right to communicate. Exactly what the right should incorporate and how it should be formulated are still far from clear. Up until now the discussions have been extremely vague and of a highly idealistic nature.

Harms, Richstad, and Kie (eds., 1977) wrote an overview of the different points that have been mentioned as essential elements of a right to communicate. They list various aspects of communication in society that may be related to the potential right. Their extensive list includes these major dimensions:

1. Everyone should have a right to get the information they need.

2. There should be an appropriate, balanced information exchange between persons, regions, and countries.

3. Information from the "outside" for culture building should be balanced by information from the "inside" of a nation.

4. Communication in the world should promote both globalism and cultural plurality.

5. The communication structure in a country should promote two-way communication at all levels.

6. People should have basic communication skills,
and they should be taught them.
7. There should be room for active participation in
society as well as individual privacy.
8. Everyone should possess a right to communication
resources to meet basic needs.

At a meeting of experts held in Stockholm in 1978 it
became obvious that there is no consensus on what the
right to communicate should include. There is not even an
agreement that such a right should be defined at all. According to some critical voices, the right to communicate
is even more basic than the human rights formulated by the
United Nations. Communication gives humankind its identity and thus it has a much more fundamental character
than even the right to shelter, clothing, or food.

Another point of criticism concerns the semantics of
the phrase. A *right* is much more than a *freedom*. It implies that someone has to ensure that the necessary preconditions for exercising such a right are fulfilled. It
implies obligations. Some critics ask: Is it really within UNESCO's mandate and scope to define these obligations
so that the right can become a powerful instrument for
improving the communication situation in, say, the developing countries?

There are more straightforward ways of approaching
the question of what the right should incorporate. Beltran
and de Cardona (1977) go to the point when they say that
the right to communicate means all human beings should
have at their disposal unrestrained options as senders and
receivers of messages carrying information and opinion.
They should have uninhibited access to sources of information. Lastly, there must exist channels through which the
individual can transmit his messages. Beltran links the
concept to the situation in Latin America today and finds
that very few of these conditions are met.

But it is unlikely that the United Nations could
formulate a right in such concrete terms as involves ownership and control of the media, and possibilities for
citizens to exercise control over decision-making processes
in society. In such a perspective it is doubtful whether
the concept will fulfill the humanitarian goals its advo-
cates claim.

Instead, there seem to be several real dangers involved in the concept and its possible future use. Just
as when the free flow principle was introduced, the question can be raised: Who can be against it? Of course,
people should have a right to speak to each other. Everyone can agree to that. But it has to be repeated: communication takes place in a social setting. Somebody sets
the bounds for the discussion, and obviously some actors

have more impact than others. Just as free flow meant a
strengthening of the positions of the already powerful,
the same pattern is likely to occur under the flag of the
right to communicate.
     The concept has to be interpreted, and this will be
done by groups in power, not by the weak or oppressed.
Limits will be fixed within which the right to communicate
may be exercised. These borders will be defined on a
political basis and will favor present power relationships
in the world. The right to communicate is not a concept
leading toward change; it is an attempt to give groups
working for liberation a feeling of being taken seriously,
while in practice the right to communicate will be used to
preserve the present order in the world and to stabilize
it even further.
     Another point of criticism should also be expressed.
If one of the most important aims of UNESCO in coming
years is to improve the media situation in the world,
particularly in the Third World, why then introduce a new
concept which only tends to obscure the picture? The
right to communicate has been given both national and international dimensions and understandably enough many
developing countries have supported the expression, if
somewhat hesitantly. They use it to describe their own
situation: they are denied the right to communicate with
the rest of the world, they have no chance in a system of
world communication dominated by a transnational enterprise system.
     The situation is thus somewhat confused. Many Third
World nations do not favor the UNESCO proposal on the
right to communicate but they sometimes find it useful to
refer to the concept when describing the international
scene of today. However, this gives the concept passive
backing and with more active interest from industrialized
countries it is likely that UNESCO will try to formulate
a definition of right to communicate as an addendum to the
Declaration of Human Rights in a few years' time. This
work must be followed with great attention.

A Third Way?
     Although the attempts to arrive at a workable defini-
tion of the right to communicate at the international level must be regarded with skepticism, this does not mean
that the concept cannot be given meaningful interpretations at the national level. The case of Sweden has received considerable attention in UNESCO after a speech de-
livered by the Swedish Minister of Education at UNESCO's
General Conference in 1974. Some observers see in Swedish
communication policy a third way--between East and West,
North and South--that might provide solutions of a more
general kind.

Although this judgment seems unrealistic and overly optimistic, the Swedish example may indicate a role for the media in which the right to communicate could be an essential and meaningful part.

Sweden has a long history of freedom of expression in the media. It was the first country to guarantee liberal freedom of the press in constitutional law. Over the years, to the extent it has been made explicit, Swedish media policy has recognized the importance of a liberal measure of freedom of speech to public debate. Another particular characteristic is that the Swedish mass media have been given different ownership arrangements.

The press is in the hands of private capital. Radio and television are owned by a public corporation, the Swedish Broadcasting Company, the shares of which are held by the major voluntary organizations in the country (temperance, evangelical churches, consumer cooperation, adult education organizations), the press, and the private industry. The general guidelines for programming are set forth every five years in an agreement between the State and the company. There is no advertising in radio or television, costs being covered by a yearly license fee paid by every person possessing a radio or television set.

Since World War II, Sweden, like many other countries, has seen a drastic reduction in the number of daily newspapers. But in Sweden the State has endeavored to see to it that the tendencies toward economic concentration in the industry are not brought to the extreme of monopolies. A subsidizing system has been introduced to secure the existence of at least two daily newspapers in major cities, where more than one have existed. This has not always succeeded, however, although the rate of newspaper failures has been dampened.

Thus, the State supports the media structure financially but does not interfere with the contents in any direct way. In a paper for the National UNESCO Commission, Hadenius and Ringdahl (1978) identify the functions the media should serve in the Swedish society:

1. A well-developed mass media structure should stimulate broad participation in society.
2. The mass media structure should strengthen national identity.
3. The mass media should give relevant information to the citizens in the country, and they should make it possible for the citizens to bring their views and opinions to the decision makers in society.
4. The mass media should function in such a way that members of the community can use the media as a forum for exchange of information and views.

5. The mass media should not only inform but also
critically examine powerful groups in society.

In this Swedish perspective the right to communicate
becomes the ability of citizens to influence decisions in
society. The media shall provide the individual with
relevant and accurate information, and thus stimulate active commitment.

But the right to communicate also means that the
media have a responsibility to give a voice to groups who
are disadvantaged in terms of their ability to make their
opinions and demands heard. Journalists working in the
media must help formulate or mediate the views of these
citizens. This is not the praxis of today, even in
Sweden, and consequently it is correct to say that the
implementation of a right to communicate requires a new
kind of journalism.

These lines of thinking concern Sweden and have
originated in this particular historical, political, and
cultural setting. Other nations may find inspiration in
this thinking, but there is little reason to believe that
this "third way" is ready for export to the rest of the
world. What the example has tried to show is rather that
if the right to communicate can be given a concrete interpretation, it may be a useful concept in changing the information flows *within* nations in the direction of more
just and equal exchanges. But it should be up to each
nation to make these interpretations, if they choose to do
so at all.

AND THE FUTURE?
Many predictions can be made but on an uncertain
basis. Quite understandably, many Third World countries
need the money they now have a chance to get. But since
they will have to buy the hardware from rich, industrialized, countries a new form of dependency will result.
The technology transfer will tend to favor the exporting
nations (Goulet 1977) and with the hardware may also come
implicit recommendations for the making of the software:
the content and style of programs and articles.

As for the transnational companies, this move will
not in any serious way threaten their positions. Rather
it seems likely that they will be able to take advantage
of this development quite well, so that the ultimate outcome will be a strengthening of their position. As a result, the small nations of the world will have to demand
a more radical departure from the status quo than they
have had to date.

Ultimately the question is: To what extent is it

possible for a small nation to create its own destiny in a world full of strong forces pressing from outside? The experience of different continents does not give reason for any optimistic view in this respect despite substantial financial aid. Instead, history shows that it takes real struggle and concerted effort to keep powerful foreign cultural elements out.

Some countries have drawn the ultimate conclusion of this and put up barriers to isolate themselves from the rest of the world at least for a time. Others have exercised strong control over both incoming technological innovations, expertise, and tourism. While these countries are very few, their endeavors have been followed with great interest by other nations in similar positions. They represent alternatives to the dominant, Western-oriented, philosophy of social change.

ADDITIONAL READINGS:

Barnet, R. J., and Müller, R. E., 1971, *Global Reach: The Power of the Multinational Corporations*. New York: Simon and Schuster

Mattelart, A., 1976, *Multinationales et systèmes de communication: Les appareleis idéologique de l'imperialisme*. Paris: Editions Anthropos.

Nordenstreng, K., and Schiller, H. I. (eds.), 1978, *National Sovereignty and International Communication*. Norwood, N. J.: Ablex Publishing Corporation.

Wells, A. F., 1972, *Picture-Tube Imperialism: The Impact of U.S. Television on Latin America*. New York: Orbis.

6
Alternative Uses of Communication—China, Tanzania, and Cuba

When Mao Tse-tung and his comrades came to Peking in 1949 and seized power over mainland China it was the beginning of a great experiment in social change that is still only in its beginning. Thirty years is a short period when looking at national development in a country the size of China and with such a long and diversified history as China's, but even so, China has already attracted great interest among the peoples of the world. Whether they express a positive or negative attitude about what is happening, observers seem to agree on one thing: the course of development that China has chosen has produced extraordinary results in a short time. China has managed to eradicate many of the ills, social and physical, that plagued the country before 1949. Although people are very poor by most Western standards of material well-being, there seems to be no starvation or malnutrition. Further, China has succeeded in sharply reducing the rate of population increase by introducing the concept of planned birth.

Such results, to which most observers attest, are remarkable in a country of such size and with such a large, ethnically mixed population. Indeed, they would be remarkable also in a small country.

Many nations look to China for solutions to their economic, political, and social problems. The questions are: What factors in the Chinese development have made it possible to attain a basic standard of living for its population? To what extent is China's experience transferable to other nations, to other political settings? And, What tasks are allotted to the media in the Chinese model, how are they carried out, and to what extent might elements of this communication model be applied in countries that follow a politically different course?

Without doubt the increased interest in China today has resulted from additional information about what has

been going on and what is going on in the country. This
increased knowledge has been brought about by changes in
relationships between China and other nations in the
world. This was particularly noticeable in the 1970s.
Other countries have similar records of conquering in
a short time some of the central problems faced by developing nations. Cuba and Tanzania, each in its own way,
probably present the most interesting examples in their
respective efforts to develop. Like China, both these
countries have attracted attention for their ways of
handling communication/education problems: Cuba for its
campaign to eradicate illiteracy, and Tanzania for its
method of using radio information campaigns to try to
solve development problems.
To understand the particular communication aspects in
the models these countries follow, we can look at the ways
in which they deviate from the dominant Western model. It
is possible then to discuss whether possibilities exist to
transfer parts of these models to other countries.

CHINA
When it is said that we now know much more than before about the Chinese experience, this is not to say we
know enough; far from it. In fact, compared to our knowledge of communication policies in many Western-influenced
countries, we know very little. The limited material
available derives from what the Chinese themselves have
chosen to pass on to the rest of the world, what foreign
visitors learn while traveling in the country, and what
observers outside China think is happening.
The scarcity of information sources means that one
has to be especially careful in drawing definite conclusions about what is really going on. Such a cautious
standpoint is all the more justified since we are dealing
with a country where choice of mode of social change is
very controversial. Much of the literature on Chinese
communication bears a negative, not to say hostile, attitude toward China's socialism. This is particularly true
of the works predating President Nixon's visit to China in
1972. Western public opinion about China, however, has
changed considerably since then, and this has brought
about less ill will in various scientific fields as well.
Nevertheless, there is still good reason to look at what
is being critically said and written about China.

Communication in China
It is clear that from the outset the Chinese revolu-
tionaries placed great importance on communication. Communication came to be used as one of the most important
tools for bringing about change in the social structure

through a broad mobilization of the human resources in the country.

Basic to the Chinese development philosophy is a specific concept of humankind. The central aim of the social transformation is the creation of a new breed of person—one directed towards collective goals, serving the people, practising moral values which promote the common good. But such a person, the reasoning goes, cannot be created and cannot exist in a society based on individual enterprise and individual ownership of the means of production. Thus, in order to bring about the needed changes in society, the people themselves must transform the social system in which they live. Men and women together must thrust off the bonds that keep them from a life of higher quality.

The work for change shall be carried out by the masses under the leadership of the Chinese Communist Party. Education of the masses to increase their knowledge of and enthusiasm for China's transformation through both the formal school system and channels which reach out to the whole adult population is a task of key importance. Only if a policy or a specific measure is in the interest of the masses and is understood by the masses, can it successfully be carried out by them.

The major impetuses for change, however, lie not in single actions by individuals or the masses. They are imbedded in the social structure system (Mao 1967, p. 5):

> Changes in society are due chiefly to the development of the internal contradictions in society, that is, the contradiction between the productive forces and the relations of production, the contradictions between classes and the contradictions between old and new; it is the development of these contradictions that pushes society forward and gives the impetus for the suppression of the old society by the new.

In China such contradictions or conflicts are seen as important motivating forces in society. As such, they are not something to be avoided as is the tendency in Western nations. These forces make it possible to identify exploitation and they show the need for new social relations. Conflicts are an unavoidable element of the development process and China has explicitly adopted a strategy of using the forces that are set in motion when a conflict is discovered and solved.

Communication between the party and the masses is intensified in processes of conflict resolution, as well. Seen from the outside, such periods may appear dramatic: sidewalk newspapers, aggressive workers using quotations from leaders to castigate and purge certain persons, mass

meetings, demonstrations. But although situations like
these may be of crucial importance, the rate of information exchange on a day-to-day basis is also fairly intensive.

Specific Features of Chinese Communication Networks

The two major elements in the Chinese communication
system are the mass media, and a net of interpersonal
channels built around small groups.

According to the political philosophy the Chinese
follow, the task of the mass media is to promote the ideas
of the Communist Party. Mass media at the national level
are consequently under the control of the party's Central
Committee. At the provincial level the party's provincial
committees exert the same control. *New China*, the official news agency in the country, supplies the mass media
with news supervised and approved by the party.

China assigns great importance to a well-developed
radio system, which is the most important mass medium.
All provinces have their own local broadcasts that reach
wide segments of the population. Considering the fact
that about one-third of the population is still illiter-
ate, radio is very important. The press, too, has an important function and is well developed. Television, however, is not given the same priority, although a system
has been in use since the end of the 1950s. Most sets are
placed in factories and day-care centers. Viewing is a
collective, not a private, activity.

But the mass media are not the most important elements in the Chinese communication system. China has a
highly developed system of groups all the way down to the
village level, and this is where the formation of social
norms largely takes place. These groups often consist of
between eight and fifteen persons, and the average Chinese
may be a member of several such groups: at his work, in
his commune or village, in a political study group.

In these gatherings, the policy of the party, as
transmitted through the mass media, is discussed, either
in general or with special attention to some aspect that
may directly concern the people in the study group. The
meetings are often held under the guidance of local party
officials, and the topics covered touch all kinds of social matters.

Empirical research has shown that small groups constitute a favorable setting for creating consensus and
common norms defining correct behavior. When individuals
who can be expected to support the official line of the
party are placed in leading positions in these groups, the
social pressure generated in the group works to support
official policies. Political study, mutual criticism, and
self-criticism are basic elements in group activity and

these may further strengthen the influence of the group on
the individual. Influence may, of course, also travel the
other way: the individual may affect the group through
criticism.
Chu (1977) distinguishes between two kinds of communication that takes place in these small groups:

1. *Normative communication*, i.e. in these groups
   norms are set on what is right and what is wrong
   in a particular situation or on a given issue.
2. *Value-oriented communication*, i.e. the study
   groups are an important tool for breaking deeply
   rooted traditional values and beliefs and replacing them with the ideological content of the
   Communist Party.

But the groups fill many other functions as well.
They are an important way of spreading literacy, and,
equally important, they provide an opportunity for people
to maintain and improve this skill. Both theoretical and
practical knowledge, particularly concerning agriculture,
are disseminated through the groups, and they provide a
natural forum for deciding on collective action to improve
living conditions in the village or province.
With the leading positions in the groups occupied by
persons actively supporting the official lines of the
party, it is possible to create a situation where people
can be mobilized to work for the ideas that the party promotes. People could not be mobilized to any greater extent, however, if it were not clear that the ideas brought
forward by the party lie in their interest. The situation
of social control represented in the study group makes it
possible to mobilize the vast majority, not just a committed few.

Other Communication Paths
We see in the Chinese communication system how local
communicators serve to create active support for the party
line, and mobilize the masses around the particular issues. At the same time these and other communicators also
relay information the other way: from the people to the
party. In this work the Communist Party has at its disposal *cadres* that serve many functions in the organizational network, among them mediating information to and
from the party leadership at various levels. In a two-way
flow of information the communication flows from party→
cadres→masses and, vice versa, from masses→cadres→
party.
In addition to this two-way vertical flow of communication, the Chinese system also relies on numerous well-
developed horizontal channels. Villages and communes

(larger administrative units) are encouraged to communicate with each other in order to improve cooperation,
especially with regard to coordinating the production of
various goods that need to be exchanged. The cooperation
is mixed with elements of competition, and the mass media
often carry stories from communes and factories that have
carried out party policies in what is considered exemplary
ways. It should be noted that local units like communes
are given great freedom in choosing how to follow the
guidelines of the party. This is part of the philosophy
of relying on the masses.

Other communes are encouraged to study the good examples the media report, and funds are made available to
permit delegations to visit such places to discuss how the
problems faced in that commune were solved. These study
trips, sometimes called *point-to-point conferences* (to
indicate that groups from different points in the country
come to one point to learn from each other) are arranged
at all levels and in all sectors of society.

It should be emphasized that the visitors are not expected to go home and copy the method used in the "ideal
commune." Rather, the idea is that they shall get ideas
which may be adapted to their own situations. An often
stressed principle in the Chinese development philosophy
is that all problems must be met in accordance with the
local conditions. There is no one best way to solve a
problem; there may be several. This is the same convic-
tion China has expressed when other countries have looked
to her for a new model for development. China has very
clearly stated that every country must find its own way.
We will return to this question later.

Campaigns
     An important characteristic of the Chinese communica-
tion system is the use of mass campaigns. Yu (1967)
claims that China has always been engaged in one or another major mass movement since 1949. But the word *campaign*
connotes information activities that are activated from
above, and this is not altogether the case in China. The
notion underlying the idea of mass mobilization is that a
campaign shall develop into a *mass movement* in which the
people take the initiative, steering the activities in the
direction they feel is important. Thus, the campaign is
only the starting point (Bennett 1976).

Mass mobilization campaigns in this Chinese sense are
carried out on a variety of topics at varying intervals.
Lindhoff (forthcoming) distinguishes the following categories according to differences in objectives:

     1. Changes in the relations of production toward a
higher degree of collective ownership.

2. Changes in the forces of production through the introduction of technological innovations, new methods of production, etc.

3. Improvements in the quality of the forces of production through reforms in health, family planning, literacy, and vocational training.

4. Campaigns aiming at ideological rectification, socialist education, self-criticism, and class struggle.

5. Changes in the social structure through increased participation in decision making at various levels.

In some cases the actual intentions and objectives of a certain campaign may be difficult to determine. A campaign that concentrates on increasing production or some other material objective may in fact deal with ideological problems.

A campaign begins with explaining the issues involved by intensive mass media coverage of the question. The people must understand the basic problems in order to carry out the studies and to take the actions the campaign aims to bring about. Local party cadres encourage people to take part in the campaign and related activities. People are also urged to voice their own criticisms of the conditions the campaign focuses on. Sidewalk newspapers have become a popular and effective way of publicizing such critiques.

Theoretical studies are carried out while the campaign lasts, but as time goes by there is an increasing emphasis on direct actions. Local activists may carry out more or less "violent" actions of various kinds directed against whomever has been defined as the "enemy" of the campaign. The cultural revolution of the late 1960s is probably the most well-known example in the West of such a campaign. Activities on the part of the masses may go on for a longer or shorter period of time, depending on the objectives of the campaign and the extent to which its goals are reached. The expected outcomes of campaigns have not always been formulated as clear-cut objectives. Due to the far-reaching decentralization of the Chinese systems, it is not possible to predict exactly what results broad mass mobilization around a certain issue may have.

An Example: Family Planning

Underlying what has been said so far is the idea that familiarity with the use of communication in China is prerequisite to an understanding of social change there. But the role of communication should not be overestimated. Many other social forces have contributed to genuinely improved living conditions: a well-balanced mixture of old and new practices, a similarly conscious balance of im-

portation of new methods and indigenous practices and
goods, an extraordinary leader (or teacher, as he called
himself) in Mao Tse-tung, and controlled population growth.
    Nevertheless, *purposive communication* has been an in-
dispensable factor. Without a well-planned strategy it
would not have been possible to win the support of the
masses and to direct them against the old structure in
society, to mobilize them toward establishing a new order.
    Purposive communication has played a particularly
vital role in family planning. This is true also in countries following a Western development model. In the latter countries communication is used to convey information
about the necessity of having fewer children and about
different contraceptive techniques. The hope is that people will realize the need for population control; that
they will see personal gains in adopting such practices.
    In China the approach has been somewhat different.
For many years after the revolutionary victory there was
only slight stress on family planning. In the Marxist
view of population growth, people are seen not primarily
as consumers, they are also potential producers. The incentives for planning population increases appeared in the
late 1950s, when the women of China were needed in the
labor force. It was also considered a question of female
emancipation and equality between the sexes.
    China has chosen to call its program in population
control *planned birth* which is different from the Western
concept of family planning. Rogers (1974) defines the
Chinese concept as including the following components:

    1. Having small families of two children in urban
areas and three children in rural areas.
    2. Spacing births at 5-year intervals.
    3. Marrying late (28 for males, 25 for females in
urban areas; 25 for males, 23 for females in rural areas).

    To win acceptance for the planned birth program, thus
ensuring that it would be carried out, the usual techniques to mobilize the people were employed. Mass media
campaigns were used, particularly in the early 1960s, and
study groups took up the issue at the local level. Perhaps even more crucial to the success of the program were
the improvements made in the health field in general. The
education of "barefoot doctors," the building of regional
hospitals, the call from the party for qualified people to
go out into the rural areas to work--all these factors
have increased the people's faith in the development of
the country and have tended to depress the birth rate.
Increased social security and health improvements lessen
the need to have large families. China has also developed
contraceptive techniques that are simpler than conventional Western ones.

The planned birth campaign is a bit different from
many other campaigns, however. The mass media have been
used to a lesser extent, and the reliance on interpersonal
channels has been greater. This may be because a campaign
of this kind takes a long time. According to several observers, there was, and still is, a lot of superstition
among the population concerning family planning. As in
many other cultures in the world many taboos are attached
to sex. So, when the mass media began to promote the idea
of family planning in the middle of the 1960s, they
aroused resentment and criticism just because they talked
openly about things that were traditionally of a private
nature.

Family planning questions came to be discussed primarily in the small groups. Respected elders were used as
leaders in the discussions, together with women members of
the cadres. An important feature of the program which has
been emphasized during recent years is that births at the
local level are decided upon collectively rather than in-
dividually. At the commune level people draw up collective plans concerning production and ideological progress;
likewise, they set their demographic goals together. They
decide which families should have children the coming
year. Priority is given to newlyweds and to couples without children.

Taken together, these are some of the main factors
that have made China's birth rate drop down to somewhere
around 1 percent, perhaps somewhat higher in rural areas.
Compared to many other developing countries this is a very
low figure.

While somewhat special in the ways indicated, the
planned birth campaign is typical of the Chinese approach
to social change in that its success stems from an interaction between purposive communication activities and
other changes that have occurred in society.

TANZANIA

Formed in 1964 as a union between Tanganyika and the
island of Zanzibar, Tanzania is a poor country with few
natural resources. One language dominates, Swahili, and
there is no single dominant ethnic group. The country has
one party, Chama Cha Mapinduzi (CCM), and it has a leader
who has come to mean much for the development of the country in a personal capacity: Julius Nyerere, reelected
President for the third time in 1975. Up to early 1977,
the name of the party was the Tanganyika African National
Union (TANU).

Tanzania follows a socialist development philosophy
under the leadership of CCM, the only official party in
the country. But CCM's ideology is not one of dogmatic
socialism. Rather, President Nyerere has declared that

Tanzania should feel free to import aspects from any system as long as it does not interfere with the country's
self-determination. Important ingredients in the system
are democratic processes, cooperative efforts, and social
change through mobilization of the people rather than co-
ercion. The Arusha Declaration of 1967 places emphasis on
development of the rural areas and on improving the lot of
the poorest segments of the population.

Popular participation in decision-making processes
plus self-reliance are two key concepts in the Tanzanian
development plan. This means eradicating the colonial
heritage and, among other things, replacing foreign personnel in top positions with Tanzanians. Such a process
is under way. It also means relying on multiple sources
of technical and financial aid, not just a few donors upon
whom the country might become dependent.

The Ujamaa villages, the basic local units in the
country, are based on cooperative production and distribution of goods. The plan is to give the villages a large
measure of responsibility in planning and other activities.
This trend toward decentralization is perhaps more a vision than a description of the situation today. Also,
many sparsely populated rural areas in Tanzania have not
yet been incorporated in the Ujamaa villages.

Communication in Tanzania

CCM is the central nerve system in Tanzania in the
sense that most major development efforts are either carried out through CCM or with its active support. Like the
party in China, CCM has used campaigns to focus attention
on particular issues in the development process. While
less systematic than Chinese campaigns, the party in Tanzania has organized and encouraged activities at the local level including both discussions and concrete actions.

The medium used most widely in Tanzanian development
efforts is radio. Tanzania has deliberately refrained
from investing in a television system so far. Radio has
an advantage in that it can reach far out in the country
at a relatively small cost. The strategy has been to com-
bine information via the mass media, particularly radio,
with group discussions and study circles at the village
level, a variation on the media forum technique mentioned
in Chapter 3. The difference is that the Tanzanian approach is much more systematic; moral and practical support is provided for by a political party with a well-
built structure nationally as well as in the villages;
only a few topics are discussed at a time; different campaigns are clearly demarcated in time.

Since 1969 Tanzania has carried out four major campaigns with the assistance of radio. Two of the largest
were run in 1971 and 1973. The first of these was to

celebrate 10 years of independence by reviewing what had
been achieved in that period. This campaign had about
20,000 participants in the radio groups.

In 1973 a campaign entitled "Man Is Health" reached
nearly 2 million. According to Hall and Dodds (1974) who
have followed the development efforts in Tanzania, the
campaign seems to have had a dramatic effect on certain
health practices among a very large number of people.
Surveys were made in several villages before and after the
campaign, and changes were noted in the buildings, use of
latrines, absence of broken pots, etc. The results show
that on the average each household in the entire sample
improved their health environment by changing two negative
health habits into positive ones. The major change consisted of the construction of pit latrines and the clear-
ing of vegetation from the immediate surroundings of the
houses. There were also indications of lower incidences
of such diseases as malaria.

Clearly, the campaign resulted in a gain in knowledge
about vital health practices among the participants. When
compared to the knowledge of control groups, the increase
amounted to about 20 percent.

Reasons for Success

The radio study campaigns produced favorable results.
These educational mobilization efforts were also positive
in economic terms since the changes that occurred used
existing technology. No new and costly equipment had to
be introduced into the villages.

The campaign approach seems to have worked for a
number of reasons. The first was the cooperation among
various governmental bodies under the auspices of the
Institute for Adult Education. Since independence, systematic knowledge about all the elements needed for good
educational efforts has been accumulated: how to produce
good material, and how to create high motivation among
teachers.

A second major factor was that the campaign was successful in creating enthusiasm and support on the part of
participants. The stress on the need for cooperative efforts to break the state of underdevelopment became an
alternative to the conventional teacher-student relationship. Furthermore, the contents of the campaign were fit-
ted into the participant's living conditions in meaningful
ways. This increased motivation to work actively in the
way the campaign suggested.

A third factor was the active role of the party in
both creating and keeping up the interest at the local
level. Through its cell system CCM is represented in most
corners of the country, and CCM members have worked for a
successful outcome of the campaigns, actively encouraging

people in the villages to participate. President Nyerere
himself made special broadcasts and has participated in
the fieldwork to create enthusiasm for the ideas that have
been promoted.
    A fourth and final factor may lie in the choice of
the campaign approach rather than institutionalizing the
themes in continuously ongoing adult education programs.
A common problem with mobilization efforts seems to be
that people's enthusiasm decreases after a period of high
participation. Tanzania has deliberately chosen to have
campaigns with clearly demarcated beginnings and ends.
Also, they have tried not to fit in too many campaigns in
a short time, although the need for increased knowledge
certainly is there. They have rather formulated their
strategy so that a long time has been devoted to planning
and coordination, then a much shorter period to the campaign itself.
    After a health education theme in 1973, Tanzania car-
ried out a similar campaign in 1975 on the theme of food
and nutrition. No results are yet available, but the general impression conveyed by some observers is positive.

CUBA
    Cuba went through a radical change when the corrupt
regime of Fulgencio Batista was overthrown, and Fidel
Castro became Prime Minister in 1959. The country declared itself socialist, and land reform, together with
nationalizations of most sectors of the economy, followed.
Education, quite naturally, was given high priority.
Adult education in the form of evening classes had existed
before the revolution, but it was almost exclusively in
the urban areas and primarily concerned with teaching
English.
    When the revolutionary government designated 1961 as
"the Year of Education," the objectives were quite different. The goal was to eradicate illiteracy which, according to official figures, was 24 percent at the beginning
of the year. The year before, Fidel Castro had "asked for
a thousand men who had education beyond the level of
second-year high school, to volunteer to go into the most
remote areas of the country to teach reading and writing,
hygiene and nutrition." Five thousand people from all
walks of life answered the call, including doctors and
engineers who had to be dissuaded from going because "the
Revolution needed them in their own professions" (Huberman
and Sweezy 1969, p. 23).
    Illiteracy was to be attacked on a broad scale in
1961. The whole population was mobilized into a teaching
force. A quarter million men, women, schoolboys, and
schoolgirls, supplied with 3 million books and 100,000

paraffin lamps, spread over the island (Werthein 1977, p. 128).

The slogan was that the people teach the people. About half the teachers involved had ordinary jobs alongside the campaign and taught 2 hours per day. The whole of Cuban society was mobilized during the 9 months the campaign lasted. Poets wrote poems, artists painted pictures and posters, composers wrote songs--all about the campaign, urging people to volunteer as teachers or enticing illiterates to join the classes. The literacy efforts became much more than just a campaign: they turned into a revolutionary cultural movement involving the whole nation.

When the alphabetization program was officially ended by the end of the year, the number of illiterates had dropped to a dramatic 4 percent. The effort in itself was a unique educational achievement compared to most other countries in Latin America, and the end result was most remarkable. Few countries at this time had less than 30 percent illiteracy.

Much more could be said about the way the literacy campaign was carried out. But it is important to understand that it was not only a campaign that disseminated reading and writing skills. It was the first mobilization effort after the revolution and the goal was to involve all Cubans, regardless of sex, age, occupation, or educational background, in a common effort to improve living conditions. The program was also to create a better understanding between people and a better understanding of the goals of the revolution. The objective was to build a base for future action in various fields of Cuban society where similar mass efforts were needed.

SUMMARY

The three examples of alternative approaches to development, China, Tanzania, and Cuba, have several things in common. All proclaim socialist ideologies, although they differ greatly in their applications of socialism. One of the most important similar traits is that ownership is collective and not individual; the means of production are either owned by the state or by some form of cooperative, as in the Tanzanian Ujamaa villages.

Likewise, all countries have but one party. They are not parliamentary democracies in the Western sense. But the process of social change in these countries is just as democratic as that going on in many other developing countries with more than one party. A host of parties is no guarantee for democracy, and neither does a single party automatically imply dictatorship. The countries discussed in this chapter have systematically worked at feeding the

hungry, providing health care and shelter for all. They
have all put the stress not on the urban sector, but more
on the rural areas where the poorest live. They have done
in action what other countries sometimes only formulate in
writing in the national 5-year plans.
But to understand how the change has been brought
about one must take into account the essential common de-
nominator of mass mobilization. In practical work, however, there are great differences among the different socialist countries.
China, Cuba, and Tanzania have proclaimed a faith in
society and in people working together. They place a
great faith in what the masses, properly guided, can
achieve. To some extent, such faith has come out of necessity. None of these countries has been endowed with
advanced technology or other riches. Their greatest asset
has been and is workpower. Mao Tse-tung very early expressed his credo on this point, saying that the people
are fundamental not only as tools for development of the
Chinese society, but that the development of the people is
an objective in itself.
What is of prime interest here is to analyze in what
ways these three countries, and possibly some others, represent other views of how the mass media and personal contacts can be used for development purposes. The following
points can be distinguished:

1. The media themselves are not seen as independent
factors for social change. Instead, they are used, where
appropriate, to contribute to the fulfillment of development objectives that are formulated for the society as a
whole. Put somewhat drastically: there is no communication policy for development, but there is a development
philosophy in which communication represents one of several parts. It is not the most important factor, but it
is absolutely necessary.
2. China, Cuba, and Tanzania all coordinate their
various development efforts more than countries following
a Western model. This is true in the field of communication as well.
3. Channels of information are to a much greater extent built up in such a way that messages may flow in both
directions, vertically between leaders and population and
horizontally between individuals and groups at similar
levels in the social stratification system.

All aspects of the organization of communication activities in China, Cuba, and Tanzania could not, of course,
be discussed here. We have only touched on some of the
most distinctive features.

TRANSFERABILITY

   We turn now to the question: To what extent can other
countries apply the communication experience of China,
Cuba, and Tanzania in their own development efforts? The
answer can hardly be given as a simple yes or no; the application depends on the level of development within the
country. It must be realized that China's, Cuba's, or
Tanzania's communication policies really cannot be iso-
lated from the development policies of each country.
Planned socialist development determines the tasks of the
communication system. The latter fits into the former,
not the other way around. Therefore, the answer must be
formulated in this way: Yes, the communication policy can
be transferred, but only if the receiving country also
imports the rest of the national policy and social organization.

   But this does not mean that other countries cannot
use *particular aspects* of the socialist experience. The
outcome cannot be expected to be the same, however. Take
family planning, for example. While it might be possible
to try using the Chinese model of collective decision making in Indian villages, can the outcome be expected to be
the same as that in China? Hardly. There are great differences between India and China politically and philo-
sophically and the idea of collective decision making is
unacceptable to many in India. That decisions about new
births should be made this way contradicts deeply held
beliefs. Nor is there any strong political force to promote such an idea. In China, land reforms and coopera-
tivization have been carried out, health services have
been improved, women have been given an equal and meaningful position in society. India has to make progress in
these areas before the Chinese experiences in joint decision making can be incorporated fruitfully.

   What about mobilization of the people? Again this
depends on the social system to which the idea is to be
transferred. Consider the case of El Salvador, for example. The kind of mobilization this country invested resources in was to expand the formal school system. It is
unlikely that El Salvador would devote efforts to the kind
of mass mobilization that China, Cuba, and Tanzania promote, and even if it did, how would the population respond?
It is very difficult to see a collective spirit of the
Cuban kind springing up in a country so explicitly based
on individual enterprise. Surely, in mass mobilization
terms it would be a failure.

   But it has to be realized that both the issues brought
up and the national setting determine the outcome of such
campaigns. El Salvador may be an extremely unfavorable
setting for such a transfer experiment. Botswana, which

does not have a socialist system, seems to have successfully copied Tanzania's radio campaigns in efforts to reduce grazing. It is too early to say anything about the
outcomes in a longer perspective, though, since the initial success may be due to a "novelty effect," frequently
noted when new media or new ideas are introduced.

The ultimate meaning of China, Cuba, and Tanzania to
other countries may be their presence as *examples* of alternative ways of development more than as sources of
specific techniques and methods. The achievements of
these three countries have provided many insights into the
mechanisms of underdevelopment and viable ways of strug-
gling to break out of such a state. Developing in a socialist way, these countries have focused attention on the
problems facing countries that try to go their own ways.
They have shown that it is possible. They have also shown
other solutions to development problems than countries
following a Western model. Thus, it is more as sources of
inspiration that they have their greatest significance for
other developing countries. As Mao has said, every nation
must ultimately find its own way and its specific design
of society on the basis of its own economic, political,
and cultural preconditions.

7
Toward a Theory of Communication and Social Change

FAILURE OF CAPITALIST DEVELOPMENT PHILOSOPHY
    Before entering this discussion, one argument should
be stated clearly. The widely felt need to revise the
dominant model of communication in social change is not
simply due to dashed hopes within the field of communication. Rather, it stems from the failure of the whole development philosophy of which the communication model is a
part.
    This is a harsh judgment which some may find too
categorical. But it is a judgment based on the experience
of the past two decades. Socioeconomic gaps between developed and developing countries are increasing instead of
decreasing; the number of illiterates in the world is
growing; health facilities in the Third World do not meet
even the most basic needs; famine and malnutrition are
still prevalent.
    It is true that several developing countries show up-
ward trends of economic growth, when this is measured in
terms of Gross National Product in total or per capita.
GNP, however, although given such an importance in discussions of living standards, shows neither *what* is growing
nor how this increase is *distributed* among different
groups in society. There is no link between growth in GNP
and the living conditions of a majority of the population.
The dominant model of development applied within the capitalist world has put heavy emphasis on investments in the
"modern" sector, in the hope that the gains made in that
sector will eventually "trickle down" to groups in the
traditional sector.
    The record, however, shows very little of such trans-
fer. Chenery et al. (1974, p. xiii) in a widely noted
book have examined the outcome of development efforts in a
large number of countries. Their general conclusion is
pessimistic:

It is now clear that more than a decade of rapid
growth in underdeveloped countries has been of little
or no benefit to perhaps a third of their population.
Although the average per capita income of the Third
World has increased by 50 per cent since 1960, this
growth has been very unequally distributed among
countries, regions within countries and socio-economic
groups.

The essential elements in what we refer to as the dominant
capitalist development model are:

1. The existence of a free enterprise system giving
transnational corporations access to both raw materials
and sales on the commercial market
2. Investments in a "modern" sector
3. Importation of advanced, capital-intensive technology by the developing country
4. Stimulation of savings by preserving income gaps,
particularly in the developing countries, the assumption
that equalization leads to less savings (= less money for
investments)
5. Development aid in the form of loans, "gifts,"
technical assistance, and trained personnel

This is not the place to go into the details of why
this model has proved inadequate with respect to improving
the living conditions of the majority of the people in
Third World countries. It is sufficient to say that some
critics characterize the model as not only inadequate but
virtually devastating to national efforts to achieve social change guided by indigenous values.
The point here is that the need for a revision of the
communication model in development arises from a convic-
tion that the dominant development model needs to be altered. The demands from the Third World for, first of
all, a New International Economic Order is one of several
signs of this need. As noted in Chapter 5, the New Information Order is part of a New Economic Order, not something that can be changed independently from economic conditions.
In an alternative model, other values than economic
growth are to be stressed. Goods and services that are
produced should be viewed as social utilities rather than
simply as items for sale. The distribution of manufac-
tured products and services is assigned equal importance.
Sometimes referred to as "the second dimension of development," equal distribution is underlined in the alternative
model. Another quality of development emphasized in alternative development thinking is self-reliance, that is,
independence from outside forces.

The question is, then, in what ways can communication
via the mass media and other channels contribute to the
fulfillment of such "new" objectives? In order to approach this problem we need a better understanding of the
role of the media in society. The dominant model has not
provided this knowledge, and so it must be reevaluated and
revised.

There is a crying need for a better theory of communication in the social change process. But the whole field
of communication suffers from a lack of theoretical con-
structs. What is present in the form of empirical data or
other experiences is a set of propositions, hypotheses,
and assumptions, while very few attempts have been made to
relate them in a theory of a more general kind.

In this chapter and in Chapter 9 some points are discussed that are needed to understand the role of the media
in society and in the changes taking place. I present no
elaborated theory, but I describe a few steps toward more
realistic thinking about communication in the development
process, in other words, a more solid foundation for such
a theory.

COMMUNICATION AND CHANGE IN SOCIETY

Scholars tend to overestimate the importance of their
own fields. Sociologists claim the necessity of viewing
problems in society from a sociological angle, economists
see the world as consisting of economic relationships, and
so on. The same is true for communicators--journalists,
researchers, administrators. In most kinds of social issues they tend to stress the role of information sent by
various media.

A prime fault in the dominant model of communication
is precisely such an overestimation of what this factor
means in the transformation process. Or one might put it
the other way around: too little importance has been given
to other conditions, and to the interaction between these
and communication.

A new perspective on communication has to begin with
the realization that change in a society includes and is
generated by a number of factors and their interactions.
The social sciences offer several different, more or less
refined theories of what moves societies forward. Evolutionary theory sees change as a gradual process consisting
of successive small steps whereas in revolutionary theory
change occurs much more dramatically. Antagonistic social
forces clash and lead to a new state of affairs, completely different from the status quo ante. Conflict is a
major element in the latter theory, while harmony is an
underlying concept in the former. In Marxist theory, the
main contradiction in society is that between the forces

of production and their negative social impact.

Communication, meaning exchange of messages between people, is present in almost all these theories. No change in society can take place without communication (other than in the case of natural disasters, floods, earthquakes, and the like). On the other hand, the outcome of the latter events cannot be controlled--the results of an earthquake cannot be foreseen!

So we may conclude that communication is present in all directed and purposive efforts to bring about change. But this does not mean that it is the most essential factor. It is only one of several components. The most important factors are those that determine the structural organization of society: the political, economic, and social conditions that set the limits within which change can occur.

Now let us get down to specifics and illustrate the role of communication and its interplay with other factors. In Chapter 3 the diffusionist approach was criticized for its neglect of structure, the rudimentary insight that farmers will not adopt new ideas and products if they do not have a real possibility to do so or if they will not benefit from it, no matter how cleverly the information has been designed. In many developing nations farmers are tenants or the land is divided into small plots. The farmer may own small pieces of land scattered over a large area. What is needed to improve living conditions and efficiency of farming in such situations (and they are common) is land reform, not information. A change in the structure is needed, not more technical know-how. This can be put in another way: information can never substitute for structural changes, no matter how ambitious the effort.

This insight is both simple and crucial and it must be emphasized since it is on precisely this point that information activities have been misused, misunderstood, and misapplied. It is meaningless to begin campaigns for better nutrition if people have nothing to eat. There is no use urging people to go to doctors, health centers, or hospitals, if they cannot be given attention due to shortage of personnel or facilities, or if they are unable to pay doctors' fees, or if they find it hard to leave their own village to travel to such distant institutions. No major result from conventional family planning campaign can be expected if living conditions are not improved or if the need to give birth to many children does not diminish.

The point should be clear by now. Communication is only one of several factors that bring about change in society. It is certainly not *the* factor. Characteristics in the structural organization of society are the major

determinants of the order of things in society. Information activities can never replace basic material alterations.
    Meanwhile, communication is indispensable to every
attempt to bring about change. Structural alterations,
for example, a land reform, require some form of coordinated efforts by people, and one of the essentials in such
joint efforts is rapport, the exchange of views and knowledge. Thus, while little change can take place without
communication, communication activities do not always result in desired change. The structural conditions have to
be right for this to occur.

Communication and Ideology

    All communication in society takes place within lim-
its set by the social organization. The goals and contents of communication are formulated within these con-
straints. Hence, the mass media are given different tasks
in socialist and capitalist societies. In a general sense
the media may be said to serve the purpose of maintaining
and strengthening the ideology that society is built on.
    In Western countries there are explicit ideas on the
functions the media are to perform. Lasswell (1948) un-
derlines the following four: news presentation; surveil-
lance; interpretation of information and presentation of
rules for action; transmission of cultural values from one
generation to another or from one part of society to another.
    Schramm (1964) used a somewhat different terminology
involving three tasks for the media: the watchman function;
the policy function; the teaching function.
    To what extent the media carry out these tasks de-
pends on several factors. But, on the whole, the con-
ceived functions of the media are to legitimize the existing social order. The media are the producers of the
social consciousness that ultimately determines people's
perceptions of the world and the society in which they
live.
    In all nations, in all social systems, the media per-
form such an ideological task. Those who control the media determine the contents with which the media should be
filled. There are great differences, however, in the degree of ideological homogeneity of the media in different
societies. In some countries there is little or no room
for viewpoints that criticize the present order of things,
whereas in others the media are more open.
    In the research literature on the effects of the me-
dia, the expression often used to describe the long-term
influence on people's ways of thinking and behaving is
agenda-sitting. The media identify the important topics
of the day, indicate how they should be thought of and

what their implications are. Since people tend to talk to
each other about what the media contain, these ways of
treating the selected topics also penetrate into the face-
to-face contacts people have. It is in the principles the
media follow in setting the agenda that the ideological
values of society make themselves visible.

Although communication is not the prime mover in social change, it is an extremely powerful instrument for
controlling one of the basic forces in society: the mental
conceptions that form people's outlooks on life. It is
not difficult to see that those in a position to control
the media can exert a decisive influence over the direction of social change.

Communication and the Media as Teachers

The overall importance of communication networks and
their contents for the organization of society is thus
clear. Now let us narrow our perspective to consider to
what extent various media contents produce effects on the
receivers.

The dominant model of communication and social change
stressed the media's role as teachers. The media are, of
course, in some respects suited to bringing knowledge to
people, but, as noted in Chapter 4, the dominant model's
faith in the power of the media in this regard must be
qualified. One must recognize that:

1. The media cannot teach people everything.
2. Even if the media are successful in teaching people new practices and ideas, there is no assurance that
this will improve the lot of the poorest members of society.

Both these points set limits as to how the media can
function as teachers. When these limits are coupled with
what has been said about communication and ideology, another constraint becomes clear. The media can teach, but
they can only carry messages that serve or do not seriously threaten the interests of these groups who control
society and the media. There is an ideological dimension
underlying the teaching of skills and attitudes.

When it comes to what the mass media can do as teachers in more concrete terms, it has to be kept in mind that
the media are essentially one-way channels. They cannot
take into account differences among individuals and groups
at the other end of the communication process--the receivers. Communicators using mass media shape their messages
so that as many as possible will grasp the contents. But
since no individual adaptation is possible, the contents
must not be too difficult. The media cannot teach many
people complicated subjects. Thus, sole reliance on the

media as teachers, while common, cannot be very effective. The media can be complemented with discussion groups--forums--but this is seldom done to any great extent. The mass media are often the only inputs in teaching efforts. This is the gist of the first point above.

The second point means that there is no direct link between the learning of new ways and a heightened living standard. While teaching via the media may be successful, it does not have the triggering effect that was anticipated. Here the problem may not necessarily lie in the media activities themselves. Instead, we should critically examine the underlying development model. Indeed, the media may work well, but they may teach people the wrong things. In such cases they help preserve the old development model, thus obstructing a course of development which might benefit a majority of the population. This is the perspective that has to be kept in mind when discussing the value of the media as sources and distributors of "new ways." The parallels to the field of education are obvious, and in the following analysis some concepts from this field will be introduced to discuss the possible effects of different educational activities.

Communication and Education

The media in their role as teachers may be looked upon as a form of *nonformal education*. Coombs and Ahmed (1974, p. 8) define this concept in the following way:

> any organized, systematic, educational activity carried on outside the framework of the formal system to provide selected types of learning to particular subgroups in the population, adults as well as children.

They distinguish this type of education from *formal* and *informal education*, which take place inside and outside a structured learning situation. Under such a definition, *nonformal* education programs include most communication efforts to teach people quite specific skills or concepts. Such programs serve both as alternatives for those who have no opportunities to acquire formal schooling and as a way of broadening the formal schooling to include new skills and knowledge.

Initiatives in the area of nonformal education may be categorized on the basis of their organization and applications of communication. First, there is the *extension approach*, which is the most conventional form. It was discussed in Chapter 3 in conjunction with the information activities interwoven into the diffusionist approach. Usually an expert or change agent informs farmers about the proper use of new seeds, fertilizers, or technological

innovations. The usual aim is to improve agricultural
productivity.
     A related variety involves the dissemination of
knowledge on other subject matters. Health, nutrition,
and employment opportunities are examples of the *campaign
approach*. The basic ambitions are the same as in the
agricultural extension approach, but the information activities often take the form of periods of intensive information activity followed by periods when little information is distributed. There are many deviations from
this general pattern, though. Health information, for
example, is put out more or less continuously, but at certain intervals extra efforts are made to improve health
conditions.
     A third form of nonformal education is the *coopera-
tive self-help approach*. The emphasis is on self-dis-
covery, articulation of needs, the building of local institutions for self-help and self-governance (Coombs and
Ahmed 1974). One country that has relied on such an approach is Tanzania, especially during the first years
after independence.
     Finally, there is the *integrated approach*. As the
label implies, it is the antithesis of piecemeal ways of
dealing with development problems. So far, however, fragmentary approaches have been the rule with specialized
governmental bodies or international agencies working with
narrow problems, paying little attention to other related
programs or the overall objectives of development. The
emphasis in an integrated approach lies in its broader
scope. Several factors related to development are included in one project: agriculture, economic aspects, literacy,
health.
     This approach requires much more national and region-
al coordination than topic-bound projects. But coordination is difficult; the more people, the more organizations
involved and the larger the probability that problems will
arise (Coombs, Ahmed, and Kale 1976, p. 81):

     Coordination bodies . . . can only be as effective as
     the degree of political commitment to and acceptance
     of integrated development and the consequent politi-
     cal and administrative ramifications. Coordinating
     bodies may also, like rhetorical pronouncements, be-
     come the subterfuge for inaction.

     Nevertheless, the integrated approach doubtless has
many advantages over the others. It rests on a development philosophy that says the solutions of problems, by
whatever methods, are more important than a concentration
on any particular factor that might offer the key to successful social change.

These are the most clear-cut categories of nonformal
education. Keeping the general limitations in mind, what
outcomes can be expected? And, are they worth the investment?

Nonformal Education as Communication

Although not all countries in the developing part of
the world assign equal importance to nonformal education,
many factors speak for its use.

First, the formal school system enrolls only part of
the population, leaving large groups, both young people
and adults, uneducated. Drop out rates are often very
high, particularly in rural areas. There is a need to involve these groups in society, and nonformal education is
one way of doing so.

Second, the learning offered in the school covers
only such basic subjects as literacy, arithmetic, geogra-
phy, and history. The people in a developing nation need
more than this unwieldy bulk of facts to take part in and
influence society. They need an adequate understanding of
contemporary events in order to improve the local and national community. In most developed countries information
about such matters is available, albeit not always easy to
find. A large output goes through the mass media, but
only a small portion of that output equips the audience to
deal with the world around them.

In the Third World it is even more difficult to gain
knowledge about the conditions in one's own country. The
books, newspapers, etc., that normally would provide such
knowledge are lacking. Travel is more difficult. A large
void is to be filled. Nonformal education activities
could help fill it; to what extent this is done depends on
the political and economic circumstances in the nation.
While nonformal education can unfold and clarify society,
it can also mystify, depending on the ideological climate
in the country.

A more concrete reason for investing in nonformal
education programs lies in their capacity to permit the
newly literate to maintain and improve their skills. This
is a great problem in rural areas in developing countries.
People of various ages acquire a functional ability to
read and write, but in an environment having few opportunities to use this knowledge the skill is soon forgotten.
In China, as noted in Chapter 6, the study group fills
this function.

Another problem is the question of equality. Primary
schools, as they function today with large groups not
entering at all, constitute one of the major stratification factors in society. A small minority is educated for
the leading posts in society, while those not entering the

school system have few or no chances to break out of their
poverty. Nonformal education programs that are particularly directed toward poor rural groups offer better opportunities to these groups. Indeed, while these programs
do not lead to any drastic changes concerning "equal opportunity for all," they can at least compensate to a
certain degree for the discrimination effected by the
school system.

Thus, the argument here is that nonformal education
is important and that it is worthwhile to go ahead with
it. But not always. One must recall what was stated earlier in this chapter: communication activities can never
be substituted for other changes. It has to be made certain that information contributes meaningfully; that it
can solve or reduce certain problems.

Consider, by way of illustration, the problem of nutrition. A communication problem may be said to exist
when food is available but people do not eat a well-
balanced diet. Likewise, there is a communication problem
if health facilities are available but people do not use
them when they fall ill. But if there are no food, no
doctors, or health centers in a region, then the problem
cannot be solved with communication. Other changes have
to be made first.

Reality is seldom as clear as these two cited situations, though. Problems are generally a mixture of structural problems *and* communication problems. But this is a
crucial point in the analysis of what communication can
accomplish: problems have to be thoroughly analyzed in
order to assess to what extent information activities are
motivated and what effects can be expected.

Effects from Nonformal Education Programs
    The question of effects has always been central in
communication research. But, seemingly, the more research,
the more complex the question appears. There once was a
time when the general view of media effects was that people exposed themselves only to content that tended to reinforce their already existing viewpoints and attitudes
(Klapper 1960). But this view is now recognized as far
too oversimplified. People's views can change by exposure
to the media, either in a short-term or long-term perspective. Many factors outside the relation, "messages in the
media--the receiver," have to be taken into account to
understand what kind of effects will be likely.

For the administrator responsible for a program in
nutrition or health, these four questions are central to
predicting outcome:

    1. What groups will have a chance to take part in
the program?

2. Of those taking part, how many will have a real chance and interest to "respond" to the program?

3. What are the chances of "learning the message"?

4. What will be the outcomes for society if the program is successful?

Further, as noted earlier, the choice of medium/media is important with respect to what kind of effects can be anticipated. The mass media can reach a large audience at the same time. The media can focus attention on particular issues and create interest for them, but they generally cannot teach people complicated matters. The reader/viewer/listener cannot ask questions, ask for clarifications, or relate the contents to his or her own personal situation.

The network of personal contacts existing in all societies have several other advantages that may contribute to the learning of more complex skills and subjects. Face-to-face contacts permit an exchange of information, repetition, clarifying of ambiguities, communication with nonverbal signs, and individual formulation of points in the argumentation.

Besides these "technical" characteristics, personal contacts also have the benefit of historical tradition. In all societies, news, entertainment, sales transactions, and cultural values have traditionally been transmitted by personal contacts. Direct contact with other persons and groups has long been the only way of getting in touch. The mass media of today have a much shorter history, and although these new media have gradually taken over many of the functions that face-to-face contacts once filled, in many cultures the personal contacts still have a higher status or at least greater trustworthiness. Such is the case in many Third World countries.

Use of media forums is intended to reap the particular advantages of both types of channels but media forums are costly and not widely used. Where media forums are not organized, another link is relied upon: opinion leaders.

In the mid-1950s the predominant view in the field of communication research was that mass media have little *direct* effect. Findings indicated that the contents of the media pass through *opinion leaders* before they reach the "ordinary" person (Katz and Lazarsfeld 1955), the most important effect thus being *indirect*. This is the *two-step flow hypothesis*. Subsequent studies have modified the hypothesis somewhat.

It is now clear that direct effects cannot be excluded. Studies among children, for example, have found strong influences among heavy consumers of radio and television. Televised violence has also been shown to influ-

ence behavior. Thus, the two-step flow has to be modified
into a *multi-step flow*. Furthermore, most people are *both*
opinion leaders and opinion followers, depending on the
topic and other factors. There is no clear-cut evidence
that some persons are always opinion leaders and some are
always followers.

Nevertheless, in many communities in developing countries leaders do exert considerable influence over the
attitudes and behavior of their people, and are thus in a
position to decisively influence the outcome of, say, a
nonformal education program. They are opinion leaders in
many areas: health, community development, agriculture.
Often their positions are based on tradition or other
vaguely defined grounds. Whatever the case, such groups
may sometimes more or less control outside attempts to
introduce change into the village.

Seen in this perspective, two-step or multi-step
flows may not result in effects in individuals in the lower strata in society. Opinion leaders will scan the mass
media looking for views and behaviors that strengthen
their own positions, first of all. Messages contrary to
their own interests may be rejected or distorted before
being passed on to others, if they are passed on at all.
New behavior in health and nutrition that might truly
benefit a majority of the population may be censored so as
to protect the vested interests of this leadership layer.

This, then, is one of several factors setting the
limits to the outcomes of nonformal education programs.
There are several others--lack of resources, little fol-
lowup at the local level, and others.

The most severe limitation of these programs is that
they reach such small segments of the populations in the
Third World. While there are great variations among nations, the general picture is clear enough to allow such
a statement. Another characteristic is their one-shot
character. People who have the chance to participate have
little opportunity to reinforce what they learn, and so
the real potential of nonformal programs is lost. The
most important impact of such programs is not primarily
what is learned in the short perspective but what this
knowledge may lead to when it comes to organizing future
activities designed to bring about more far-reaching improvements.

How Can Nonformal Education Programs Be Improved?

Keeping in mind that education programs do not in
themselves carry any magic keys to improved life quality,
they do represent certain possibilities. Consequently, we
have good reasons for trying to make them work better and
for trying to reach those groups who have the greatest
need for what the programs can teach.

As has been said, if the mass media are to be used at all, they should be coupled with personal channels, even if this means greater expenses. Contacts have to be established with elders and traditional leaders so as to get them to accept the ideas the program is promoting, or at least to see that they do not actively work against them.

The schema (shown in Figure 7.1) summarizes the general pattern of communication flows.

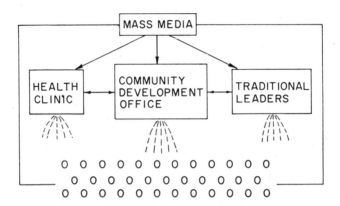

People in the village

Fig. 7.1. Plan for a nonformal education program

The main emphasis should fall on the local level and personal contacts. The mass media have a supporting function. Often nonformal education programs are run only in some specific regions or villages. Then, local mass media (to the extent that such media exist) have to be used in the supporting role. A key word is *coordination* among the various levels and the timing between mass media messages and local activities.

But however well the cooperation between authorities is organized, the key problem is motivating the people to participate in the program. Motivation can only be increased if the programs become better adapted to the conditions and needs of the people. This requires a greater degree of influence on the part of the people over such programs. The *top-down development philosophy* with which almost all programs are imbued can never be quite successful. The objects of development--the people--have to be made into subjects.

One way of increasing people's preparedness to exert such influence is to stimulate their contacts with each other. Nonformal education programs (vertical communication) should always try to initiate horizontal communication between people (the base of the figure). In this way

these programs can become tools for self-organization and
for bringing future activities better in line with actual
conditions.

Communication as Complement

Communication should complement other measures. In
other words, when a change is made in, say, the legal relation between landowner and tenants (for example, a new
law is passed increasing the rights of the tiller), this
must be made public. At least, it has to become known by
those affected. The landowner will most surely learn
about it. But for those working in the fields this is
far from certain. Information explaining and interpreting
the provisions of the law must be brought to them. This
is the meaning of the complementary role of communication.

This particular function of communication has been
treated by the United Nations Development Program and has
been given a special label, "development support communication." It refers to the use of communication in aid
projects to explain the aims of the project to the people
the project will affect. The hope is that this will improve the chances of success of such programs. The idea
is well founded, but since it in practice means only information *from* the authorities to the "grass-roots," it can
only bring about very limited improvements. It amounts to
an extension of the dominant top-down development thinking
and gives people little chance to work out suitable projects themselves.

In a more general sense, however, the complementary
function is crucial, not least in its negative form. Consider the hypothetical situation in which government is
trying to improve material conditions for the poor, while
privately owned mass media campaign against the measures
proposed. Here we have not "support communication," but
a case of *hostile complementary communication.* The record
shows that the vested interests behind such hostile media
campaigns may be so influential as to be able to pigeon-
hole bills and block the implementation of legislation.

8

New Perspectives on Development—How Can Communication Contribute?

Many of the countries now called the developing countries once had civilizations and politics of high standing in human history. The fortunes of nations, however, and the political and economic relations between them have changed, and as a result of colonialization by European powers and later others, the peoples of Africa, Latin America, and Asia have been thrust into a state of dependency. Nations having at last won their political freedom find it extremely difficult to shape their own futures. Prevailing political, economic, and military relationships in the world today still favor the industrialized nations, many of which are the former colonial powers.

DEVELOPMENT DEFINED

Against such a background it is easy to understand why many choose to see development as a process of liberation. Goulet (1971, p. xx) gives a broad definition of what the term should mean:

> freeing men from nature's servitudes, from economic backwardness and oppressive technological institutions, from unjust class structures and political exploiters, from cultural and psychic alienation--in short, from all of life's inhuman agencies.

This leaves room for varying interpretations, but, at any rate, it says something about what development is not. Developmental progress cannot be measured with but one or a few indicators, such as GNP, GNP/capita or degree of industrialization. Rather, development in this perspective implies a process whereby the overall personalities of the peoples of the Third World are rehabilitated and strengthened after years of dehumanization. It is just as much a development of humankind as it is a development of material living conditions.

These two aspects are naturally closely linked. Newly independent nations have inherited an economic structure designed to function in an era of colonial rule. The
aim of the colonial economy was to satisfy the needs of
the colonizing country and a small minority in the colony
while the large majority of the colonial population lived
in poverty and starvation.

In most countries the heritage after independence was
an economic organization ill suited to the needs of the
majority of the population. But it was also something
much more. Colonial rule damaged and destroyed the values,
practices, and organizations that had been developed over
hundreds of years in harmony with the surrounding environment. The new social and economic relations imposed from
outside resulted in an alienation of people from their
original and natural potentials. Consequently, in the
underdeveloped countries, people were forced into identi-
ties that hindered the full use of their latent powers.

Thus, one of the most urgent goals in the development
effort is the dealienation of human beings. Dignity,
self-respect, faith in one's own capabilities, the creation of a consciousness about one's own importance in the
process of change in society--all these are essential elements in a theory of development.

Today there is an intense discussion on what the term
development should imply, and what specific values should
be given priority. The background for this has been
sketched previously: the failure of the capitalist development philosophy. As a result there is a general search
for "another development" (Nerfin, ed. 1977), and inspiration for such ideas comes from various sources. China,
Cuba, and Tanzania, briefly discussed in Chapter 6, are
three countries that have chosen alternative paths to
development. At this writing several other nations are
also in the process of staking out yet other alternatives
to Western models of development, among them Angola,
Somalia, Guinea-Bissau, Mozambique, and Vietnam.

In this chapter some aspects of this reorientation in
development will be examined more closely, and the focal
questions are: How can communication contribute to the implementation of these newly emphasized values? Or, How
does communication *not* contribute? The following four
aspects have been selected for analysis: self-reliance;
participation; equity in distribution; a new rural development and leadership.

These particular ideas have gained wide acceptance as
essential features of a "new development." They have also
become so popular that although a country may not want to
change the overall development orientation, it wants to
complement it with one or several of these goals. To some
extent rhetoric is involved, but the fact remains that in

these four dimensions are some of the most generally pro-
fessed components of a new development.
So the question is: What can communication do with
regard to the realization of these values?

SELF-RELIANCE
Reliance on importation of advanced technology from
abroad, while it may bring about development in the traditional sense more rapidly than can an indigenous social
change, decreases the possibilities of self-determination
and creates new forms of dependence.
The idea of self-reliance stresses the use of locally
available raw materials, simple production processes, and
application of indigenous know-how accumulated over the
years. This thinking has been further stimulated by some
recently published writings; perhaps the most well-known
is E. F. Schumacher's *Small Is Beautiful* (1973).
Many advantages are inherent in such an approach
quite aside from a lessening of foreign influence:

1. It makes use of the great surplus of workpower,
which so far has had few alternatives in rural areas. In
most Third World contexts an appropriate technology is one
of low capital intensity but high labor intensity.
2. It takes advantage of existing knowledge, thereby
diminishing the need for mass educational information campaigns on how to use a new technology.
3. It creates job opportunities in rural areas.
4. It can be more useful in the sense that the commodities produced can be adapted to fill local needs. It
is different from large-scale technology, which mass
produces standardized products not suited to specific uses.
5. It promotes the idea of cooperation and the notion that one person, together with others, can do something about the problems facing a village or country.

The revival or introduction of an appropriate technology cannot solve all the problems of poor countries,
however. And, in many cases, large-scale technology is
necessary to produce the goods and infrastructures needed
to make production with appropriate technology effective.
It is important to point out that locally adapted production is not a nostalgic idea of going back to stone axes
and similar instruments of production. It is a way of
utilizing existing resources, both human and material, in
a better way.

Communication and Self-Reliance
Self-reliance in the development effort demands a
dialogue, an exchange of information, between the people

and the leaders. This has major implications with respect
to the organization of communication activities. The
country that imports technology and know-how from abroad
has to invest much in training and education in how to
use these imports; "traditional top-down flows" in the
terminology used above. But, when raw materials, technology, and knowledge are available in the country, the
question becomes one of how best to *share* these resources.
To resolve such a question, there must be channels from
the people (who possess the knowledge of how to use these
assets) to the local leaders and to other people in the
village. In the terms used earlier, there has to be
vertical communication, initiated from below, and horizontal communication.

Self-reliance means a greater use of workpower. A
strengthening of the collective spirit is necessary to
make labor intensive efforts work. Communication structures designed to stimulate this spirit must be created.
It is much more a question of "doing things together" than
traditionally. (This is also the title of one of the few
books that discusses communication and the use of appropriate technology; Fuglesang 1977.)

The forming of group thinking has to be reflected in
the *contents* of the communication. Statements of leaders
professing their faith in the people may sound pretentious,
but how else can cooperative efforts be encouraged? The
problem is not only to find the technical solutions suited
to a local village, but it is equally important to find
ways of stimulating people to work together.

The practical organization of communication activities can take many forms. One that was tried on a small
scale at a Tanzanian-Swedish project concentrated on local
communication centers. In the region of Arusha in Tanzania the ideas of self-reliance and appropriate technology were actively promoted. When a specific task (for
example, the construction of a latrine of a particular
design) was carried out, the steps in the process were
documented on tape in the course of the project. Cassettes with sound recordings on a variety of subjects were
filed in the communication center. Villagers are now able
to check out cassettes and a simple recorder whenever they
want to draw upon the experiences gained in the project.

In this way local knowledge is being used, and the
center acts as a place for the exchange of information between those who have expert knowledge (the project personnel) and those who know what resources are locally available. In this sense the project represented a diversion
from the top-down communication model discussed earlier.
It was an "information exchange" model. In the Tanzanian
model the problem was not to persuade people to do something, although those sponsoring the project quite natu-

rally hoped that people would find the material available
at the communication center useful and would apply it on a
broad scale in the area.

This is only one example of how communication activities can be practically organized at the village level in
order to promote self-reliance. Other emerging nations
around the world share a common desire to break the top-
down streams of information. The key word is *sharing*.

PARTICIPATION AND LIBERATING EDUCATION

In Chapter 7 we noted that *one* (certainly not the
only one) reason why nonformal education has not been successful is simply that the contents have not been well
adapted to the needs and demands of the participants.
Consider this simple communication model:

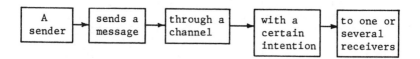

If in such programs the receivers were better able to
influence the sender(s), the outcome would surely be
better.

Lack of influence on the part of receivers is a problem of far greater generality, however. A commonly recognized fault in many development efforts in the Third World
is precisely the fact that the receivers of assistance
have been given little chance to actively participate in
the decision-making processes preceding and during the
projects.

Participation is an important ingredient in the rec-
ipe for sound decisions. It increases motivation and people's interest in their own communities and their nation.
Participation means dialogue; it means that decisions are
not taken until those immediately concerned have had a
chance to express their views and opinions on the matter.
Otherwise, the implementation of a centrally made decision
may run into difficulties due to the decision's inadequacies or because the people affected by the decision have
not enough insight into the problem at hand.

History shows many examples of the opposite, however.
Oppressive regimes have been able to stay in power, even
though they hindered participation. Or, more precisely,
they persist *thanks to their suppression of popular influence*. But dictatorships are bound to go under for this
very reason. The leaders get further and further from the
mind and will of the population, and when they no longer
have any support, they fall.

Thus, we may say that the popular participation is a prerequisite for decisions that have a chance of being successfully implemented over the long run and of gaining response from the people. Participation is liberation, or at least an essential element of it. But there are no simple ways of increasing participation. Many traditions of collective decision making were destroyed by the colonial powers.

School systems built up by foreign powers according to foreign patterns were one of the chief instruments for introducing the hierarchical decision-making processes of the West. Thus, many developing countries today have school systems ill adapted to their situations. The example from El Salvador referred to now and again in this book is a case of a nation that has tried to change the thrust of its school system. Such examples are few, however. In the vast majority of Third World countries, the main function of the school is to select officials for private management and public administration. During the last decade or so criticism of educational contents and institutions in the Third World has mounted. Illich (1970) is one such critic. Another is Freire (1970a, 1970b, 1973) whose ideas are particularly interesting in this context since he presents alternatives to the present system which conceives of education as a process of liberation.

The basic idea is that education must give people tools by which they can understand and change society. Only then will people be really motivated to learn such skills as reading and writing. In Freire's program, education is just as much a question of shaping social consciousness as it is learning to master some specific skills or techniques.

In addition to participation, Freire's model stresses the need for cooperation with others. In what ways can communication, under present or altered conditions, achieve full participation or at least increase participation relative to the situation of today?

Participation and Communication

Generally speaking, participation requires that people be given an opportunity to speak their minds. There have to be communication channels to make this possible, but in the world today this does not appear to be the case. Very few channels lead *into* the mass media, and "ordinary people" have little chance to influence the contents of the media.

These problems are not unique to the developing countries. In Sweden, where increased involvement is recognized as a goal by all political parties, the established mass media have offered few opportunities for such participation. Instead, other channels have been created and other steps taken to help increase active commitment; for example, legislation, and new views of what constitutes legitimate political struggle. Indirectly, however, the media have had to adapt to the general trend toward increased participation in society. They have had to cover such participation in their programming and articles.

The media represent a potential which can act in either of two ways: for increased participation or against it.

Let us consider the increased participation view first. In their selection of news items and programs and through a certain mode of presentation the media can stimulate interest in societal matters. The media can give individuals knowledge that will increase their understanding of the community. In turn, this will give them a greater chance of exerting control over their environments. As a result, motivation to participate increases.

Likewise, the mode of presentation is important. How are things phrased? A newspaper article can be written in several ways. Facts can be presented as "God-given" or, less authoritatively. Questioning the present order of things encourages receivers to "mentally" take part in the communication process. They may find they need to know more about a certain topic, and need to discuss the article with others.

In this way the media can assist in creating a positive climate for participation. They can provide people with relevant and action-oriented knowledge, and they can also show ways to channel such interest.

But let us not be overly idealistic! To say that the mass media *can* do these constructive things is not to say they in practice will. They may well endeavor to do exactly the opposite, to *thwart* all attempts at increasing participation. In the world there are many examples of this.

What the media will do is determined by the context in which they exist. Just as in the case of ideology, political, economical, historical circumstances are the decisive factors. Whether participation will be promoted or prevented is an ideological question of great importance. It deals with exactly how society should be built--in a dialogue with a majority of the population or not?

Here we have stressed the important role of the media. Many developing countries are trying to increase the active interest of the people in order to arrive at "better" decisions on all levels of society. The media are among the keys to the success of such efforts.

EQUITY IN DISTRIBUTION
     As was said in Chapter 7, the dominant, capitalist
model has failed to close the gaps between the developing
and developed countries. Instead, these have widened.
The same result is true within many poor countries. The
introduction of technological means of increasing productivity and the organization of cooperatives and credit
unions have not benefited all farmers and workers to the
same extent.
     Those with traditionally strong positions in society
have been the ones to gain from such a strategy. They
have had the necessary financial means to utilize the new
and often costly machinery, fertilizers, and crops. They
have been able to dominate organizations meant to serve
the interests of the small farmers. This is another illustration of the general principle that those who possess
something at the outset have greater chances of acquiring
more of the same than those who have little.
     There is now a greater stress on distribution aspects
in development, especially in the discussion of "another
development." Some industrialized countries such as
Sweden stipulate that their technical assistance programs
must try to achieve a fair distribution of economic and
other benefits in the recipient society. The criterion is
that the poorest shall gain.
     In the communication field, too, there is a growing
concern about equity. For example, how should media output be used by different groups in society? From the general principle stated above, it is clear that initial differences may be further strengthened by information flows.
Knowledge feeds knowledge, and knowledge is the basis for
social action. If equity is to be promoted, the widening
of such gaps in knowledge and other resources must be
checked.

Communication Gaps
     Figure 8.1 shows in a schematic way the discussion of
two groups in society. At a given point in time (t_0),
Group 1 knows more about, say, family planning than Group
2. The aim is to reduce the difference between the groups'
knowledge of the subject. To close the gap, family planning information is prepared and disseminated through such
channels as adult literacy classes and radio forums. Then
at a later point in time (t_1) the knowledge of the two
groups is again measured. Most likely, at least this has
been the outcome in several studies both in the Third
World and in other settings, both groups have increased
their knowledge. But the group who had the best initial
knowledge has now come into an even more favorable position compared to the low-knowledge group. The difference
between them has increased. Here we have a communication

effects gap, in this example measured in terms of a difference in knowledge.

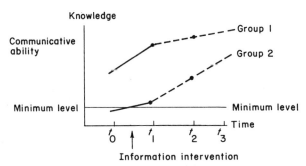

Fig. 8.1. Communication effects gaps

But although gaps do occur in a short time perspective, they may close or at least narrow if the perspective
is extended somewhat. One reason for this lies in the
following theory. An important function of the mass media
is that they set the agenda for what is being discussed
by members in society. It takes some time for issues to
trickle down to reach large groups in society. If, however, the media devote a lot of attention to an issue,
sooner or later the issue will also appear on the agenda
of these groups. When it does, Group 2 will also learn.

When the family planning issue reaches Group 2, the
contents and the form of the original information may have
changed considerably. This is inevitable since long communication chains also mean distortion. In most cases
such distortion has undesired effects, but there are also
advantages. The message, the language used, become better
adapted to the particular group that constitutes the audience. It may well be that the initial campaign message
was ill suited to Group 2; that the way of presenting the
various family planning techniques was not at all in line
with the needs or problems that people in this group felt
were relevant. Over time, however, the interpersonal network has acted upon the message to give these persons a
better chance to understand the meaning of the family
planning ideas.

At point t_3 the difference may have decreased even
further. Katzman (1974) argues that gaps will always exist in a society, but the criteria will vary over time.
As old gaps close, new ones will open up in an ongoing
process. In Sweden 100 years ago, few people knew what
parties were in the Parliament. Today most people know,
but other knowledge differences have emerged.

A second point must be considered when discussing
gaps: gaps may not be the crucial problem at all. Some-

times it is desirable that everybody in the population
possess a *minimum* level of knowledge. In that case the
gaps, if they do occur, are a lesser evil. In terms of
the figure this would mean that the major objective of the
information activity between t_0 and t_1 is to lift Group 2
over the minimum threshold level of knowledge. In the
case of family planning this may mean a general understanding and acceptance of the concept and a knowledge of
one practical technique.

Given this goal, the figure shows a case of success.
Group 2 is over the minimum threshold after the campaign.
The gap between Groups 1 and 2 has increased, but for the
time being this is not of prime concern. Another terminology could be used to express this important outcome:
we might say that the difference between the two groups
at point t_1 is *quantitatively* larger than at point t_0, but
it is *qualitatively* smaller. This qualitative dimension
of knowledge should be given the most attention.

This brings up a third question: What is knowledge?
This is by no means an uncontroversial concept--it has to
be defined by someone. And in measuring the effects of
particular information activities, or the continuous
"normal" output of information, the construction of items/
questions to measure knowledge always reflects a value
orientation on the part of the "interviewer." People tend
to acquire information and knowledge adequate for their
own situation. Hence, different groups in society have
different kinds of knowledge. Most surveys and other
kinds of studies are blind to this fact, however.

Indeed, one may wonder about some of the results concerning communication gaps. Group 1 can be called a
"better-off" group, while Group 2 is "worse-off." The
researchers conducting the study most likely belong to
better-off groups themselves, and this influences their
way of defining knowledge. If researchers belonging to a
worse-off group had carried out the study--an unlikely
situation, however--the knowledge measures may have looked
quite different.

On the topic in focus here, Group 1 and Group 2
probably have quite different perceptions as to what
knowledge is relevant. Giving birth to many children may
be rational for the worse-off group in that it gives
some form of social security, which Group 1 can get in
other ways. But rejection of family planning does not
. count as the "right" knowledge as defined by authorities.

How Can Communication Gaps Be Avoided?
      The discussion above has attempted to place communi-
cation effects gaps in a larger perspective. It has been
pointed out that many of the gaps that seem to be increasing tend to decrease in the long run. But new gaps

open up as old gaps shrink. Conventional measures of knowledge are not always to the point; the knowledge gaps discovered must always be related to the character and the subjectively perceived relevance of the knowledge being measured.

This is not to say that gaps do not exist. On the contrary, wide differences between groups or classes exist in both developed and developing countries, and differ ences are manifested not only in knowledge gaps. In the field of communication there are great variations in individuals' abilities to *find* relevant information, to *understand* it, to *use* it. This is the most important aspect of communication gaps, and it can be summarized in the term *communicative ability*. Such factors have not been studied as much as knowledge, but they are quite evident. The Swedish scholars Nowak, Rosengren, and Sigurd (1977) are among the few to have examined the matter closely.

With this broad definition of communication gaps in mind, we turn to the question of how such differences can be avoided through the use of mass media to disseminate information. This is an important problem which merits further attention both in developed and developing parts of the world. A more even distribution of opportunities and the ability to communicate (receive and impart information) is not only a worthy goal in itself for reasons of equity. It is also an essential precondition for broad popular social participation, a key objective of "another development."

Now we are no longer dealing with narrow information problems or communication *effects* gaps. The changes implied go beyond these boundaries: a society with greater equality between people, education for all, a recognition of everybody's right to participate in decision making in society.

While the kind of alterations needed to reach these objectives obviously extend beyond the field of communication, changes in the media themselves may also reduce the differences discussed here.

The essential point is that information activities disseminated by the mass media and other channels have to be designed specifically for the least advantaged members of society. All groups cannot make use of the same message. If a country wants to bring about equality between people, more resources have to be devoted to the poorest/ weakest groups.

Examples. Some of the cases in which this theory has been tried in practice are encouraging. In a report of a field experiment with television and agricultural knowledge in India, Shingi and Mody (1976) conclude that information

(in this case via telecasts) can narrow initial differences in knowledge, provided, however, that the information activities are particularly adapted to the needs of
the low-knowledge group. The language used, the symbols
and examples, all have to be designed with this group in
mind.

Other agencies are continuously attempting to use the
media to narrow differences between groups in society.
One of the best known is Acción Cultural Popular (ACPO), a
Catholic church-supported organization in Colombia.
Acción Cultural Popular aims directly at the poorest
groups in society, seeking to stimulate economic progress
among the *campesinos* through opportunities for self-
improvement. Participation in local and community organization and the creation of a critical consciousness are
other essential objectives.

Acción Cultural Popular uses a multi-media approach
to reach these groups: radio broadcasts, a weekly newspaper with a very high circulation, low-cost textbooks.
Acción Cultural Popular also operates training institutes
for its field staff, relying heavily on radio broadcasts
supplemented by written material. The organization seems
to have achieved considerable success. Basic skills such
as literacy have been acquired by many farmers. Other im-
pacts are more difficult to assess, but according to circulation figures of the rural weekly paper and books, ACPO
seems to get a good response among the poor. There is
also evidence, however, that landowners have been more
prone than the landless to adopt innovations promoted in
the radio schools (Coombs and Ahmed 1974). So as gaps
narrow in one area they may widen in another.

With its systematic direction of efforts to the weakest in society, ACPO is an interesting case. A similar
example is the Puebla Project in Mexico. The site of the
latter project is an area inhabited by farmers with lots
of small size farms and little or no opportunities for
capital investments. The goal of the project is to find
ways of improving the situation for these groups of farmers. The project deliberately concentrates on disadvantaged groups and it does not work with farmers who already
are a bit better off. Thus, it tries to bring about increased equality in society.

The Puebla Project approaches the farmers through
extension agents. These organize various meetings, discussion groups, and local credit groups. Much of the information conveyed concerns the growing of especially
developed seeds (maize and beans) and the formation of
cooperatives.

The results of the project are mixed and show some
of the problems facing groups trying to get out of a socially deprived situation. One such problem concerns far-

mer participation in credit unions. During the first 3 years of the project enrollment increased sharply, but then the curve turned downward, only a few of the potential members having joined. One possible explanation revolves around the concepts *opportunity cost* and *risk-taking*. Many of the nonjoining farmers were dependent on the cash incomes they could make on other temporary employment, besides farming their own plots. If they were to join the credit unions, get new varieties of seeds and possibly also invest in some agricultural technology, they would have to devote much more time to farming and thus would have to give up their cash earnings. Doing so would put them in a much riskier situation since agricultural production in the area is very dependent on weather conditions.

Despite the difficulties, Puebla and ACPO show that it is possible to plan information/communication activities in such ways that not only the "better-off" will benefit. But it takes astutely planned and concerted efforts. It is not enough to simply prepare some nonformal education programs, transmit them, and hope for the best. One must begin with the needs of the weakest groups and adapt all information output to their capacity to make use of it.

To repeat: inequalities in knowledge or ability to communicate are a reflection or a symptom of other socio-economic inequalities. Hence these latter inequalities have to be attacked in order to bring about equality in the communication field.

This does not prevent our declaring that all attempts to minimize communication gaps should be supported. Indeed, a strengthening of the ability of the weakest groups to handle information may be an important prerequisite for other, more basic changes to be brought about. It may give these groups the tools to get organized and to formulate their demands for better living conditions--to become a political force in society.

RURAL DEVELOPMENT AND LEADERSHIP

Four Asian scholars, Haque, Mehta, Rahman, and Wignaraja (1977) connected with the United Nations Asian Development Institute in Bangkok, have presented an outline for a strategy of rural development in Asia that summarizes many of the ideas implicit in "another development." It is presented in a special issue of the journal *Development Dialogue*, published by the Dag Hammarskjöld Foundation in Uppsala, Sweden. The authors express visions of both long-term social progress and short-term changes, and they offer some concrete examples. They see the transformation of rural areas and people living out-

side the cities as the basis for successful change.
     But their road to development is hardly conflict-free
or painless. To free the forces embodied in the rural
masses, these have to be given much greater possibilities
than now to influence decision making in society. The
authors use the concept *participatory democracy* to describe the ideal situation.
     Change in society has to be brought about by the
landless and landpoor, but since these groups have been
oppressed a great many years, they need the inspirational
power that only committed leadership can give. The progress attained must then be consolidated and institution-
alized. Otherwise, there is a great risk that situations
after a time will revert (Haque et al. 1977, p. 50): "Evidence is clear from history that gradualist and piecemeal
efforts at social change, even if genuinely motivated,
backslide into the hands of the vested interests."
     In some respects, these ideas have been brought up
earlier in this chapter. The quoted book brings together
much of the criticism that various scholars have raised
against the dominant model for development. A key expression is "develop your own way," used to underline the
necessity of genuinely original change, not the importation of "package deals."
     Consequently, it would be a mistake to dismiss this
Asian model as a revolutionary model. Instead it should
be seen as an alternative approach to development, con-
taining both revolutionary and reformist ideas. The
stress on increased democratization and participation is
in line with current thinking both in developed and Third
World countries. What distinguishes the cited work from
other approaches to the subject, however, is its concrete-
ness. The explicit emphasis on rural areas and on the
quality of leadership are also two prominent features,
although not really new. This brings us to the question
of communication in rural areas, and again the question
is: What can communication do?

Communication, Rural Development, and Leadership
     Most media in developing countries are concentrated
in the urban areas. This is where the educated groups
live, where the highest number of literates is found,
where the money is. Rural areas generally have a much
poorer mass media structure. Thus, if the aim is to promote development in rural areas, change is required. Different media are more or less well suited to serving rural
areas. Radio is an inexpensive and far-reaching medium
with a great potential for carrying development-related
contents. Television, on the other hand, is costly, demands considerable technical equipment, and cannot transmit signals far without relaying stations.

In other words: the communication setup has to be
oriented toward rural areas; the contents have to be made
relevant not only to urban groups but to rural workers and
farmers as well. Even more important, however, is that
people in these areas be given a chance to influence the
programs and contents. It is a question of letting these
groups control the media themselves, instead of having
them remote-controlled from the cities.

The same applies to leadership. Communication structures have to be created in such ways that people not only
feel but actually *are* responsible for their own development. The concept of participation has been stressed
through the last chapters. Development in a "new" perspective is not something that can be imposed from above.
It has to be the result of a mutual interplay between
leadership and the masses, in which the latter make up the
potential force and the leaders act as pathfinders seeking
out channels through which the force can be exerted.

To make this interplay work, there have to be channels for information exchange. There are no magic formu-
las for how information should flow, and it is difficult
to carry such a discussion further without taking into
account differences between countries, regions, villages.
There is also another risk involved. In written plans,
many nations today rank both rural development and active
involvement high on their list of development objectives.
In this book there is no reason to get involved in development rhetoric. The aims stated are clear and their
realization into practical action is a problem that must
be solved by the people concerned. To give more specific
recommendations here would be to degenerate into a pater-
nalistic behavior, which certainly does not rhyme with
new development; it is part of the old dominant model.

9
Need for Dialogue

In Chapters 7 and 8 some basic and specific observations
were presented as contributions to a better, more realistic, more coherent theory of communication in social
change. As has been indicated throughout this book, the
field is in dire need of a new theory based on more scientific findings, not the false and simplistic assumptions
underlying the model that has been predominant to date.

A new model cannot be expected to win acceptance simply by virtue of its scientific superiority, however. As
noted in Chapter 2, the communication strategy implied by
the old model has strong political overtones. Interests
that want to preserve the basic economic and power relationships in the world today would find it useful to keep
control in the hands of the industrialized countries. A
new model that might lead to a weakening of these power
relationships would be met with resistance no matter how
much sounder or more scholarly the model was conceded to
be.

The best way a new theory can become accepted is by
showing its superiority in practice--its ability to predict the outcomes of practical undertakings. This requires continuous discussions between researchers and
planners of communication activities in developing countries. As was said in the Introduction, contacts between
scholars and administrators have been sadly infrequent and
fraught with misunderstanding.

Clearly, cooperation is needed to exchange experiences and to collaborate in rendering existing theories
more valid. Only through such joint efforts can the new
perspectives on the role of communication in social change
be advanced.

A dialogue between researchers and planners can also
be fruitful in another sense. To arrive at a good theory,
an interplay between the construction of concepts and relationships on the one hand and reality on the other must

take place. The construction of valid theories requires
competent research. An exchange among theorists and
practitioners must develop a plan as to the kind of research that is needed. In making such outlines, both
groups can contribute by identifying problems and areas of
research relevant to both. This aspect has been largely
missing to date. It is another gap to be filled, or at
least not allowed to be widened further.

In this final chapter some views on the conduct of
research on communication problems in developing parts of
the world are discussed. They are to be seen as a complement to the building blocks for the new theory presented
in Chapters 7 and 8. Some general, more methodological
problems are examined also, and possible areas for relevant research are identified.

GROWING IMPORTANCE OF RESEARCH
Over the years the general view of research has slowly changed. Research is no longer seen as primarily a
form of academic exercise. The usefulness of scientific
investigations is now a widely applied criterion, and the
need for them is widely recognized. One reason for this
shift in attitude is that new forms of research have
emerged, forms better equipped to deal with complex realities. Some of these are briefly mentioned below. They
are examples of the kinds of research that should be encouraged since there are clear potential benefits to both
planners and researchers.

First, two forms of investigations deviate in their
approach from more classical assumptions on how research
should be carried on.

The first goes under the label *action cum research*.
It means that the researcher does not place himself or
herself as a passive observer outside the arena of activities. Instead, he or she initiates and takes active part
in the change process, while following and documenting all
relevant events as accurately as possible.

The second approach, which relates to the action cum
research role, is referred to as *participatory research*.
The basic idea here is that no research can be carried out
free from values. All research and all stages in the
research process--selection and definition of problems,
choice of design, and measurements--reflect the values and
interests of certain groups in society. Since the resources and potential to carry out research are in the
hands of the most powerful groups, little or no research
has been carried out that begins with a concern for the
interests of the poorest in society. Participatory research is a positive correction of this prevailing situation. As the name implies, the researcher participates in

a local village or region, studying problems *from the perspective of the weakest groups.*

Both these forms of research are interesting, since
they present new opportunities. Research does not have to
be carried on with especially constructed experimental
control group designs which are usually quite hypothetical.
Instead, investigations can be made in conjunction with
applied activities wherein the research team can be counted as a resource since its members can assist in the implementation of the program at hand.

This approach offers great opportunities for elabo-
rating actions and research programs in such ways that
both planners and scholars can benefit from them. It is
a distinct asset that planned activities and research can
be carried on within a common framework, not as two sepa-
rate procedures.

This potential for cooperation is easily available in
several problem areas; it is simply a question of formulating the issues to be investigated in the right ways.
One such area is *evaluation.* Communication program results need to be evaluated with respect to what they accomplished. Did they reach the goals they were supposed
to?

Such studies were earlier looked upon by administrators with suspicion since they were seen only as a control.
A contributory fact was that the practical research was
done by one group of people and the evaluation by another
group--an "evaluation team" of experts called in from the
outside.

Today a change of attitude can be seen, although it
is occurring slowly. More resources are now allocated to
measuring the outcome of specific programs, and the concept *formative evaluation* has gained acceptance. This
means that small-scale evaluations are made as the communication program develops. Thus, evaluation is integrated into the normal project activities. This permits
the administrator to change the course of the program if
early evaluations show that something is not working as
planned. In such cases it is obvious that people in official executive positions and researchers can benefit
from each other's views. To a great extent it is a question of envisioning research in a new way and of giving
researchers new tasks.

Methodological Issues

As the role and functions of research change, great
efforts must be devoted to increasing the quality of research in the Third World. Over a longer time-order,
research institutions in Africa, Asia, and Latin America
must be strengthened and there must be cooperation between
these and the developed parts of the world.

But there is also need to improve the quality of the
research now being carried out by both Western and Third
World scholars. One may even question many of the generally accepted findings on which the discussion today is
based. The methods used for collecting data have been so
crude and so influenced by different sources of error that
the value and the applicability of many findings seem extremely doubtful.
     Rogers et al. (1976, p. 17) make the astute observa-
tion that:

> a social scientist's perception of problems . . . is
> structured by the concepts and theories that he has
> been taught. He sees status, alienation, fatalism
> and achievement motivation because he has been taught
> these concepts. And, of course, he does not perceive
> phenomena for which he lacks concepts. So his scien-
> tific language structures or limits, his perceptions
> of the world, and it affects his choice of concepts,
> theories and methods for investigation.

Western Bias
     This is the first and possibly most serious source of
error. "Social science" has always meant "Western social
science," and the various theories, concepts, and definitions of problems virtually all originate in the West.
This means that research issues have been formulated
there, and concepts and theories have been transferred to
other settings without much heed paid to historical and
cultural differences in various parts of the world. This
is another expression of the domination of the West in the
field of communication--research. This bias is reason
enough to question many of the results reported. How do
we know that questions formulated in the West and investigated in countries with completely different conditions
and traditions are really the most important and pertinent
ones? How do we know that concepts and variables evolved
in one part of the world have any meaning when applied to
different cultures?
     Ways to meet these difficulties are seldom even dis-
cussed, let alone discussed at any great length. Rogers
et al. (1976) offer a simple example to show how cross-
cultural equivalence can be reached. They take social
status (an often used variable in Western research) as an
illustration. Whereas the classic indicators of status in
the United States and Europe are formal education, position at work, income, or some combination of these; in
communities in, say, Africa, other operational measures
have to be applied. Number of wives or number of horses
owned might be the appropriate indicators there. Whatever
the case, the appropriate indicator(s) must be identified

before the main study is carried out if an acceptable degree of cross-cultural conceptual equivalence is to be
attained.

As has been said before, this question has been
shamefully neglected, albeit with some exceptions. Without too much exaggeration, it can be said that Western
researchers have made trips to underdeveloped parts of the
world, collected their data under heavy time pressure, and
gone home. By necessity little time has been devoted to
such issues as those discussed above. Consequently, we
have good reason to be skeptical of the results.

Better Methodology Needed

A great need for improvements to raise the overall
quality of the research exists in the collection of data
in surveys and field experiments. In many studies it is
absolutely necessary to draw a random sample of persons
to be interviewed in order to make generalizations appli-
cable to a larger population. But how can such a subgroup
be selected when no population statistics exist or when
they exist in sparsely populated areas with poor roads?

The common solution has been to draw other kinds of
samples. This is only natural, since time and cost have
been pressing factors. One method has been to enumerate
the accessible households in the area, select some of
them, and interview whatever adult happens to be at home.
Other variations have been used. Few studies have used
the random samples necessary to give the results a wider
interpretation.

The collection of data in the Western interviewing
situation is not without its particular difficulties
either. Often it is extremely difficult to make sure that
the respondent really understands a question that may have
been formulated first in, say, English, and then translated into the local language. The very choice of words
may be crucial. Then there is the assumption that people
will respond as individuals. Such an assumption is often
doubtful, since in many local cultures the community is
based on the family and collective decision making.

These questions, too, have largely been overlooked.
And no wonder, we might add. Once Western researchers have
managed to collect their data, they usually tend to down-
play the limitations their studies may have. Quite naturally they are more prone to talk about the importance of
their results.

Thus we may conclude that what is needed is better
methodology. Although the topic has been discussed only
sparingly, some works are now appearing. Two of these are
Pausewang (1973) and Kearl (ed., 1976), who discuss in
detail the theoretical and practical problems that the
social science investigator meets and suggest solutions to
them.

No highly elaborated methodology, costing large sums
of money, is being called for here, but if research is to
be meaningful, if the resources spent on investigations
are to bear any fruit, certain basic conditions and criteria have to be met. These demands are generally accepted. The fact that the research is carried out in a
"developing" context is not an excuse for using a methodology of such poor quality that the results cannot be
meaningfully related to the social problem in focus.

Research Priorities

To improve the chances of cooperation between communication researchers and administrators responsible for the
planning and execution of communication activities, it is
necessary to open a concrete discussion of appropriate
topics for scientific study. This is mostly a problem of
setting priorities, since it is not at all a difficult
task to identify problems. The idea here is to make an
inventory of issues that fall into the category of relevant research.

The suggestions that follow are by no means exhaus-
tive. They are to be regarded as an extension of the main
ideas that have been presented in this book. In striving
to develop the new models of communication and social
change already under way, the concept of development toward liberation is central. The problem is to elaborate
a communication strategy that fits into the new development philosophy with its prime emphasis on attaining freedom from all forms of dependence.

Research is needed to develop such a theory, but the
problems selected for study must also be of relevance to
decision makers in the developing countries. In short,
the research to be given priority should be of a pragmatic
and decision-oriented kind.

Bearing these different criteria in mind, the various
research topics have been grouped into four nonmutually
exclusive categories.

General Questions

1. What is needed, first of all, is better overall
knowledge of the role of media in different settings.
Ideally, such studies should be undertaken so that the
results from various countries (developed or developing or
regions within a country) are easily comparable. These
experiences will increase our understanding of the functions the media serve under different conditions, and in
what ways they are related to social change phenomena.

2. Related to this first point is the need to examine communication policy planning in detail. Most countries lack comprehensive, clearly articulated policies for

their communication activities (Ploman 1977). There is little or no coordination between the various branches and sectors of society that are engaged in the production, organization, and dissemination of information. These may even strive in opposite directions, toward contradictory objectives.

The problem, evidently, is to find means by which national communication plans can be formulated to fit the overall plans of the country, its economic and social goals. Analyses of this problem should treat such issues as control over the media, objectives for communication activities in theory and practice, coordination possibilities between various bodies responsible for these purposive programs.

3. In the discussions on a New International Information Order, several particular problems have to be given a much closer examination. The Commission for the Study of International Communication Problems has dealt with them to some extent, but the work of the commission has to be complemented with independent scientific studies, particularly studies focusing on the following questions:

--The relations between a New International Information Order and a New International Economic Order;
--The problem of creating general public awareness about the demands for a new order in the world;
--The role of transnational companies in the communication fields with regard to their domination in news dissemination, advertising, computer techniques, satellites, and consulting services, and the consequences of their hegemony over the world's communication facilities.

Questions for Research in the Third World

1. Earlier in this book, it was pointed out that one grave criticism that could be raised against communication activities in developing parts of the world, was that they followed Western, commercially oriented models. This has also been one of the prime reasons for their limited success. There is a need to supplant these approaches with other models better adapted to local conditions and the needs of the population. Several scholars and administrators, among them Diaz Bordenave (1976), have stressed this point.

2. In the work toward developing newer, more appropriate ways of conveying information to and from the people, all existing channels have to be examined, not only modern mass media. Traditional forms of exchanging information through personal contacts should not be put aside. These play a central role in local communication

systems. The interrelationships between the mass media
and channels developed through a long chain of handed-down
traditions should be studied closely.

3. In the perspective of development as liberation
brought forward in Chapter 8, the stress is on development
on the rural areas. This is the order of priority adopted
in several countries. One problem, however, is that most
media are concentrated in urban centers. Research has to
be carried out to indicate possible arrangements by which
rural newspapers, radio broadcasts, or other media can be
employed for development purposes.

4. Although there is general knowledge of the ex-
ternal domination of communication channels in Third World
countries, we lack thorough knowledge of the consequences
of such domination for individuals or the society as a
whole. A related question is: How can a small country
take part in true cultural exchange with other nations
without being penetrated by potent alien values?

5. The difficulty of finding ways to implement a New
International Information Order has been mentioned above,
but one particular problem that has special relevance to
Africa, Asia, and Latin America should be taken up here,
namely the difficult and sensitive matter of journalism
training. A "new order" in the field of information puts
new demands on the working journalist; "a new kind of
journalism" is often talked about and was discussed in
Chapter 5. But how can such hopes be fulfilled in the
Third World, where there are few training institutions,
and where the few that exist follow the same lines as
journalism schools in the West? The problem is even
greater, since many working journalists in the Third World
have actually received their training in Europe or the
United States. How can viable alternatives with respect
to both institutional arrangements and the contents of the
training be prepared?

6. As a last point in this section, let us also consider some more general questions for research which relate to the communication strategy for liberation discussed in Chapter 8. How can communication be organized
so as to increase participation, achieve self-reliance,
promote equity, and close communication gaps? The answers
given earlier are not specific enough to lead to direct
actions (they are to be regarded more as guidelines) and
additional detailed studies are urged.

Questions Concerning the Exchange between Developing and
Developed Countries

1. Researchers and practitioners must seek out ways
to create alternative channels to complement or replace
present ones characterized by the one-way flow described

in Chapter 5. Such channels are needed not only in the
field of news, but also, for example, in the area of culture, if international exchange is to take place on a basis of mutuality rather than dominance-dependence relationships.

2. Technological aspects are as important in the
field of communication as in many other sectors of society.
New technology is available, which to many developing
countries is most inviting. But the installation of new
telephone linkages, computer systems, electric typewriters,
and copying machines creates a dependence of a new kind.
Spare parts and service are needed, and in introducing
such technology a certain organization of society is imported, too. The consequences of such technology transfer
from industrialized to developing countries have to be
analyzed more, so that dependency can be avoided or mini-
mized. Not only the consequences, but the whole process
leading to such decisions should be analyzed closely.

3. It is now clear that the industrialized countries
are prepared to extend financial assistance toward the
strengthening of mass media facilities—the result at
UNESCO's General Conference in Paris in 1978. These aid
programs should be closely examined. Much optimism has
been expressed about the outcomes of these effects. This
is strongly reminiscent of the great expectations of the
early 1960s. But will these interventions really contribute to the shaping of better, more equitable situations
in the field of information? The best way to find out is
to make formative and summative evaluations.

Methodological Questions

To improve the quality of research, a number of methodological problems have to be carefully examined.

1. Considerable time and effort must be devoted to
the choice of the most appropriate ways of observing, asking, surveying, and sampling. Sometimes small methodological excursions are called for. There is a need for innovative research to solve problems which today look hard to
crack. A marked conservatism has prevailed in the choice
of research techniques when conducting surveys or experiments in Third World milieux. Scientific tools must be
chosen with respect to the problem to be approached, and
scientific analysis of the problem is needed in order to
produce good techniques.

2. One particular area that has been seriously
underrepresented is economic analyses. The reason is
partly methodological; it is simply very difficult to
estimate costs accurately. But, for the administrator,
financial aspects of future or past communication activi-

ties are crucial: How should a limited amount of money be
used? What yields most for the dollar?
       The crucial problem is that the cost of a project is
not always the same as the sum of the outlays. Economists
instead use the "opportunity cost" or the true cost for
society; in other words, the value the resource would have
in its best alternative use. For example, suppose three
different national learning systems, each employing a different number of teachers in the school, are being compared. In each system, the cost of teachers is not the
sum of their salaries, but what they might contribute to
the economy if they were employed in other capacities.
       In economic analyses such concepts as cost-effective-
ness (the relation between input and output) and cost-
benefit (the relation between cost and benefits to society)
are also central, but they need to be clarified and heu-
ristic, pragmatic advice given to the financial decision-
makers to provide easier ways of calculating costs.
       A last point to be examined is how cost data should
be recorded and kept. This is a great problem for the
evaluators, who must consult all kinds of sources, and yet
may not find everything they need. As a consequence, cost
evaluations in many Third World countries have to be regarded with skepticism--a situation that should be altered
through research and practical action.
       3. The final point on the list of problems of high
priority is the organization of research itself. The
question is: How to obtain the best possible results?
Should research institutions in developing countries be
independent bodies, should they be connected to a university, or should they be part of the governmental ministerial organization?
       There is no simple answer, and surely the particular
conditions in each country should determine the optimal
setup. This is also true for the second major problem
under this heading: How should research cooperation with
the developed countries be structured so as to achieve research of good quality, while not extending the dominance-
dependence relationship between these two parts of the
world?

AND, FINALLY . . .
       This journey into the land of world communication is
now approaching its end. But the discussions are only in
their beginnings. Over the coming years this debate will
continue, most likely with increasing intensity.
       The priority given by UNESCO to communication is one
indication of this trend.
       The open ideological confrontations between countries
and interest groups is another.
       The great problems of reaching international agree-

ments concerning communication satellites, the distribution of radio frequencies, and so forth, is a third.

Consequently, we have several reasons for keeping a critical eye on what is happening in the communication field over the coming years. The Third World is about to receive financial assistance for the building of mass media infrastructures and we should follow the outcomes of this. Considerable optimism is expressed about what this will lead to, but idealistic thinking should now be outmoded. The experiences of the past twenty years or so show that hopes are one thing and practical outcomes quite another. Sometimes they bear no resemblance whatever.

It is appropriate to put our faith in the media. But that faith should be anchored in the political realities of the world today. This is also the major criterion for formulating a more realistic theory about communication and social change.

REFERENCES

Baran, P. A., 1957, *The Political Economy of Growth*. New York: Monthly Review Press.

Baran, P. A., and Hobsbawm, E. J., 1961, "The Stages of Economic Growth: A Review." *Kyklos* 14:234-42.

Baran, P. A., and Sweezy, P. M., 1966, *Monopoly Capital*. New York: Monthly Review Press.

Barnet, R. J., and Müller, R. E., 1974, *Global Reach: The Power of the Multinational Corporations*. New York: Simon and Schuster.

Beltran, L. R., 1974, "Communication Research in Latin America: The Blindfolded Inquiry." In *Scientific Conference on the Contribution of the Mass Media to the Development of Consciousness in a Changing World*. Leipzig: Karl Marx Universitat.

Beltran, L. R., 1976, "Panel Discussion on Research, Policy and Alternatives." In Chu, G. C.; Rahim, S. A.; and Kincaid, D. L. (eds.): *Communication for Group Transformation in Development*. Honolulu: East-West Center, East-West Communication Institute.

Beltran, L. R., and de Cardona, E. F., 1977, "Communication Rights: A Latin American Perspective." In Harms, L. S.; Richstad, J.; and Kie, K. (eds.): *Evolving Perspectives on the Right to Communicate*. Honolulu: University Press of Hawaii.

Bennett, G., 1976, *Yundong: Mass Campaigns in Chinese Communist Leadership*. China Research Monographs, No. 12. Berkeley, Calif.: Center for Chinese Studies.

Boyd-Barrett, O., 1977, "Media Imperialism: Towards an International Framework for the Analysis of Media Systems." In Curran, J.; Gurevitch, M.; and Woollacott, J. (eds.): *Mass Communication and Society*. London: Edward Arnold and the Open University Press.

Brown, M. R., and Kearl, B. E., 1967, "Mass Communication and Development: The Problem of Local and Functional

Relevance." University of Wisconsin: Land Tenure
    Center Paper No. 38.
Carnoy, M., 1974, *Education as Cultural Imperialism.* New
    York: David McKay.
Carnoy, M., and Levin, H. M., 1975, "Evaluation of Educa-
    tional Media: Some Issues." *Instructional Science*
    4:385–406.
Chenery, H.; Ahluwalia, M. S.; Bell, C. L. G.; Duloy,
    J. H.; and Jolly, R., 1974, *Redistribution with
    Growth.* London: Oxford University Press.
Chu, G. C., 1977, *Radical Change through Communication in
    Mao's China.* Honolulu: University Press of Hawaii.
Coombs, P. H., and Ahmed, M., 1974, *Attacking Rural
    Poverty: How Non-Formal Education Can Help.* London:
    Johns Hopkins University Press.
Coombs, P. H.; Ahmed, M.; and Kale, P., 1976, "Communica-
    tion and Integrated Rural Development." *Media Asia*
    3(2):81–86.
Diaz Bordenave, J., 1976, "Communication of Agricultural
    Innovations in Latin America. The Need for New
    Models." In Rogers, E. M. (ed.): *Communication and
    Development: Critical Perspectives.* Beverly Hills,
    Calif.: SAGE Publications.
Dorfman, A., and Mattelart, A., 1975, *How to Read Donald
    Duck: Imperialist Ideology in the Disney Comic.* New
    York: International General.
Elliot, P., and Golding, P., 1974, "Mass Communication and
    Social Change: The Imagery of Development and the
    Development of Imagery." In de Kadt, E., and Wil-
    liams, G. (eds.): *Sociology and Development.* London:
    Tavistock Publications.
Evans, P. B., 1972, "National Autonomy and Economic Devel-
    opment: Critical Perspectives on Multinational Cor-
    porations in Poor Countries." In Keohane, R. O., and
    Nye, J. S. (eds.): *Transnational Relations and World
    Politics.* Cambridge, Mass.: Harvard University Press.
Felstehausen, H., 1973, "Conceptual Limits of Development
    Communications Theory." *Sociologica Ruralis* 13(1):
    39–54.
Frank, A. G., 1967, "Sociology of Development and Under-
    development of Sociology." *Catalyst* 3:1–67.
————, 1969, *Capitalism and Underdevelopment in Latin
    America.* New York: Monthly Review Press.
Freire, P., 1970a, *Cultural Action for Freedom.* Cambridge,
    Mass.: *Harvard Educational Review* and Center for the
    Study of Development and Social Change.
————, 1970b, *Pedagogy of the Oppressed.* New York:
    Seabury.
————, 1973, *Education for Critical Consciousness.* New
    York: Seabury.
Frey, F. W., 1973, "Communication and Development." In

Pool, I. D., and Schramm, W. (eds.): *Handbook of Communication.* Chicago: Rand McNally.

Fuglesang, A., 1973, *Applied Communication in Developing Countries. Ideas and Observation.* Uppsala: Dag Hammarskjöld Foundation.

————, 1977, *Doing Things...Together.* Report on an Experience in Communicating Appropriate Technology. Uppsala: Dag Hammarskjöld Foundation.

Golding, P., 1974, "Media Role in National Development: Critique of a Theoretical Orthodoxy." *Journal of Communication* 24(3):39-53.

Goulet, D., 1971, *The Cruel Choice: A New Concept in the Theory of Development.* New York: Atheneum.

————, 1977, *The Uncertain Promise. Value Conflicts in Technology Transfer.* New York: IDOC, in Cooperation with the Overseas Development Council.

Grunig, J. E., 1971, "Communication and the Economic Decision-making Processes of Colombian Peasants." *Economic Development and Cultural Change* 18:580-97.

Guback, T. H., 1969, *The International Film Industry.* Bloomington: Indiana University Press.

————, 1974, "Film as International Business." *Journal of Communication* 24(1):90-101.

Hadenius, S., and Ringdahl, J., 1978, *On Communication Policy in Sweden.* Stockholm: Swedish National Commission for UNESCO.

Hall, B., and Dodds, T., 1974, *Voices for Development: Tanzania's Radio Study Group Campaigns.* Cambridge, England: International Extension College, Cambridge University.

Harms, L. S.; Richstad, J.; and Kie, K. (eds.), 1977, *Right to Communicate: Collected Papers.* Honolulu: University Press of Hawaii.

Havens, A. E., 1972, "Methodological Issues in the Study of Development." *Sociologica Ruralis* 12:252-72.

Haque, W.; Mehta, N.; Rahman, A.; and Wignaraja, P., 1977, "Towards a Theory of Rural Development." *Development Dialogue* 2:7-137.

Hoselitz, B. F., 1960, *Sociological Aspects of Economic Growth.* Glencoe, Ill.: Free Press.

Huberman, L., and Sweezy, P. M., 1969, *Socialism in Cuba.* New York: Monthly Review Press.

Illich, I., 1970, *Deschooling Society.* New York: Harper and Row.

Inayatullah, 1967, "Toward a Non-Western Model of Development." In Lerner, D., and Schramm, W. (eds.): *Communication and Change in the Developing Countries.* Honolulu: East-West Center Press.

Inkeles, A., and Smith, D. H., 1974, *Becoming Modern. Individual Change in Six Developing Countries.* Cambridge, Mass.: Harvard University Press.

Katz, E., 1973, "Television as a Horseless Carriage." In
    Gerbner, G.; Gross, L.; and Melody, W. (eds.): *Com-
    munication Technology and Social Policy: Understand-
    ing the New "Cultural Revolution."* New York: Wiley.
Katz, E., and Lazarsfeld, P., 1955, *Personal Influence.*
    Blencoe, Ill.: Free Press.
Katz, E., and Wedell, G., 1977, *Broadcasting in the Third
    World. Promise and Performance.* Cambridge, Mass.:
    Harvard University Press.
Katzman, N., 1974, "The Impact of Communication Technology:
    Promises and Prospects." *Journal of Communication*
    24:47-58.
Kearl, B. (ed.), 1976, *Field Data Collection in the Social
    Sciences: Experiences in Africa and the Middle East.*
    New York: Agricultural Development Council.
Kincaid, D. L.; Park, H-J.; Chung, K-K; and Lee, C-C,
    1975, *Mother's Clubs and Family Planning in Rural
    Korea: The Case of Oryu Li. Case Study 2.* Honolulu:
    East-West Center, East-West Communication Institute.
Klapper, J. T., 1960, *The Effects of Mass Communication.*
    Glencoe, Ill.: Free Press.
Lasswell, H. D., 1948, "The Structure and Function of
    Communication in Society." In Bryson, L. (ed.): *The
    Communication of Ideas.* New York.
Lerner, D., 1958, *The Passing of Traditional Society.*
    Glencoe, Ill.: Free Press.
Lindhoff, H., forthcoming, *Mass Campaigns and Mass Move-
    ments in China.* Stockholm: Economic Research Insti-
    tute.
McAnany, E. G., 1973, *Radio's Role in Development: Five
    Strategies of Use.* Clearinghouse on Development Com-
    munication: Information Bulletin No. 4.
McClelland, D. C., 1961, *The Achieving Society.* New York:
    Van Nostrand.
Mao Tse-tung, 1967, *Quotations from Chairman Mao Tse-tung.*
    New York: Bantam Books.
Mattelart, A., 1976, *Multinationales et systèmes de com-
    munication: Les appareleis idéologiques de l'imperi-
    alisme.* Paris: Editions Anthropos.
Mayo, J. K. (ed.), 1976, *A Critique of Development and
    Communication Trends in Tanzania, the Ivory Coast,
    and El Salvador.* Stanford, Calif.: Institute for
    Communication Research, Stanford University.
Mayo, J. K.; Hornik, R. C.; and McAnany, E. G. (eds.),
    1976, *Educational Reform with Television: The El
    Salvador Experience.* Stanford, Calif.: Stanford
    University Press.
Mayo, J. K., and Spain, P. L., 1977, *Communication Policy
    Planning for Education and Development.* Conference
    Report. Stanford, Calif.: Institute for Communica-
    tion Research, Stanford University.

Nerfin, M. (ed.), 1977, *Another Development: Approaches and Strategies.* Uppsala: Dag Hammarskjöld Foundation.

Nordenstreng, K., and Schiller, H. I. (eds.), 1978, *National Sovereignity and International Communication.* Norwood, N.J.: Ablex Publishing Corporation.

Nordenstreng, K., and Varis, T., 1974, *Television Traffic-- A One Way Street?* Paris: UNESCO Reports and Papers on Mass Communication, No. 70.

————, 1975, "The Non-Homogeneity of the National State and the International Flow of Communication." In Gerbner, G.; Gross, L.; and Melody, W. (eds.): *Communications Technology and Social Policy.* New York: Wiley.

Nowak, K.; Rosengren, K. E.; and Sigurd, B., 1977, *Communication, Privilege and the Realization of Human Values.* Interim Report from the Research Survey, "The Individual in the Information and Communication Society: Communication, Social Organization, Human Resources." Stockholm: Committee for Future Oriented Research.

Nypan, A., 1970, "Diffusion of Innovations and Community Leadership in East Africa." Paper presented at the Seventh World Congress of Scoiology, Varna, Bulgaria.

Pausewang, S., 1973, *Methods and Concepts of Social Research in a Rural Developing Society: A Critical Appraisal Based on Experience in Ethiopia.* München: IFO - Institut für Wirtschaftsforschung, Afrika-Studienstelle. (Afrika-Studien, 80)

Petrusenko, V., 1978, *A Dangerous Game: CIA and the Mass Media.* Prague: International Organization of Journalists.

Ploman, E. W., 1977, "Communications Policy Planning." In Teheranian, M.; Hakimzadeh, F.; and Vidale, M. L. (eds.): Communications Policy for National Development. London: Routledge and Kegan Paul.

Pool, I., 1963, "The Mass Media and Politics in the Modernization Process." In Pye, L. W. (ed.): *Communications and Political Development.* Princeton, N.J.: Princeton University Press.

Pye, L. W. (ed.), 1963, *Communications and Political Development.* Princeton, N.J.: Princeton University Press.

Rao, Y. V. L., 1966, *Communication and Development.* Minneapolis, Minn.: University of Minnesota Press.

Rogers, E. M., 1962, *Diffusion of Innovations.* New York: Free Press.

————, 1974, "Communication for Development in China and India: The Case of Health and Family Planning at the Village Level." Paper prepared for the Summer Program of Advanced Study on Communication and Development. Honolulu: East-West Center. University Press of Hawaii.

Rogers, E. M., 1976, "Where Are We in Understanding the Diffusion of Innovations?" In Schramm, W., and Lerner, D. (eds.): *Communication and Change: The Last Ten Years--and the Next.* Honolulu: East-West Center. University Press of Hawaii.

Rogers, E. M. (ed.), 1976, *Communication and Development: Critical Perspectives.* Beverly Hills, Calif.: SAGE Publications.

Rogers, E. M.; Ascroft, J.; and Roling, N. G., 1970, *Diffusion of Innovations in Brazil, Nigeria, and India.* Lansing: Michigan State University, Department of Communication.

Rogers, E. M.; Eveland, J. D.; and Bean, A. S., 1976, *Extending the Agricultural Extension Model.* Stanford, Calif.: Institute for Communication Research, Stanford University.

Rogers, E. M.; Niehoff, A. H.; Sen, L. K.; van den Ban, A.; and Hursh, C. G., 1976, "Research for Development." In Hursh, C. G., and Roy, P. (eds.): *Third World Surveys: Survey Research in Developing Nations.* New Delhi: Macmillan.

Rogers, E. M., and Shoemaker, F. F., 1971, *Communication of Innovations: A Cross-Cultural Approach.* New York: Free Press.

Rostow, W. W., 1960, *The Stages of Economic Growth.* Cambridge, England: Cambridge University Press.

Schiller, H. I., 1976a, *Communication and Cultural Domination.* New York: International Arts and Sciences Press.

————, 1976b, "Advertising and International Communications." *Instant Research on Peace and Violence* 6(4): 175-82.

Schramm, W., 1964, *Mass Media and National Development. The Role of Information in the Developing Countries.* Stanford, Calif.: Stanford University Press, and Paris: UNESCO.

————, 1967, "Communication and Change." In Lerner, D., and Schramm, W. (eds.): *Communication and Change in the Developing Countries.* Honolulu: East-West Center, University Press of Hawaii.

————, 1977, *Big Media, Little Media: Tools and Technologies for Instruction.* Beverly Hills, Calif.: SAGE Publications.

Schumacher, E. F., 1973, *Small is Beautiful: Economics as if People Mattered.* New York: Harper and Row.

Shingi, P. M., and Mody, B., 1976, "The Communication Effects Gap: A Field Experiment on Television and Agricultural Ignorance in India." In Rogers, E. M. (ed.): *Communication and Development. Critical Perspectives.* Beverly Hills, Calif.: SAGE Publications.

Somavia, J., 1976, "The Transnational Power Structure and

International Information. Elements of a Third World Policy for Transnational News Agencies." *Development Dialogue* 2:15-28.

Spain, P. L.; Jamison, D. T.; and McAnany, E. G., 1977, "Radio for Education and Development: Case Studies." A document of the Education Department of the World Bank.

Tunstall, J., 1977, *The Media Are American. Anglo-American Media in the World.* London: Constable.

UNESCO, 1961, *Mass Media in the Developing Countries.* A UNESCO Report to the United Nations. Paris: UNESCO.

———, 1963, *Statistical Yearbook.* Paris: UNESCO.

———, 1975, *World Communication.* Paris: UNESCO.

———, 1978, International Commission for the Study of Communication Problems. Interim Report on Communication Problems in Modern Society. Paris: UNESCO.

University of Tampere, 1973, Proceedings of the Symposium on the International Flow of Television Programmes, University of Tampere, Finland.

Varis, T., 1973, "International Inventory of Television Programme Structure and Flow of TV Programmes between Nations." University of Tampere: Institute of Journalism and Mass Communication.

———, 1976, "World Information Order." *Instant Research on Peace and Violence* 6(4):143-47.

Wells, A. F., 1972, *Picture-Tube Imperialism: The Impact of U.S. Television on Latin America.* New York: Orbis.

Werthein, J., 1977, *A Comparative Analysis of Educational Television in El Salvador and Cuba.* Stanford, Calif.: Stanford University Press.

Wilson, J. Q., 1973, "On Pettigrew and Armor: An Afterword." *The Public Interest* 30:132-34.

Yu, F. T. C., 1967, "Campaigns, Communications, and Development in Communist China." In Lerner, D., and Schramm, W. (eds.): *Communication and Change in the Developing Countries.* Honolulu: University Press of Hawaii.

INDEX